SpringerBriefs in Computer Science

SpringerBriefs present concise summaries of cutting-edge research and practical applications across a wide spectrum of fields. Featuring compact volumes of 50 to 125 pages, the series covers a range of content from professional to academic.

Typical topics might include:

- A timely report of state-of-the art analytical techniques
- A bridge between new research results, as published in journal articles, and a contextual literature review
- A snapshot of a hot or emerging topic
- An in-depth case study or clinical example
- A presentation of core concepts that students must understand in order to make independent contributions

Briefs allow authors to present their ideas and readers to absorb them with minimal time investment. Briefs will be published as part of Springer's eBook collection, with millions of users worldwide. In addition, Briefs will be available for individual print and electronic purchase. Briefs are characterized by fast, global electronic dissemination, standard publishing contracts, easy-to-use manuscript preparation and formatting guidelines, and expedited production schedules. We aim for publication 8–12 weeks after acceptance. Both solicited and unsolicited manuscripts are considered for publication in this series.

**Indexing: This series is indexed in Scopus, Ei-Compendex, and zbMATH **

Artem Kruglov • Giancarlo Succi

Developing Sustainable and Energy-Efficient Software Systems

Artem Kruglov
Innopolis University
Innopolis, Russia

Giancarlo Succi
Università di Bologna
Bologna, Italy

This work was supported by Innopolis University and the Russian Science Foundation (Grant No. 19-19-00623)

ISSN 2191-5768   ISSN 2191-5776   (electronic)
SpringerBriefs in Computer Science
ISBN 978-3-031-11657-5   ISBN 978-3-031-11658-2   (eBook)
https://doi.org/10.1007/978-3-031-11658-2

This Springer imprint is published by the registered company Springer Nature Switzerland AG
The registered company address is: Gewerbestrasse 11, 6330 Cham, Switzerland

Anna,
Hoc opus tibi dedico.
Amor est vitae essentia.
Giancarlo

Preface

An important research priority for the study of sustainable systems is the development of modeling and decision-making approaches that support dynamic, adaptive management rather than static optimization. This requires methods for understanding the full implications of alternative choices and their relative attractiveness in terms of enhancing system resilience. Due to the complexity of coupled systems, researchers should explore the simultaneous use of multiple models that reflect different system interpretations or stakeholder perspectives. In these circumstances, it is essential to analyze, monitor, and forecast the values of the basic parameters of the system, which directly affect its efficiency and sustainability.

A number of technical advances will likely improve the usefulness of models, including rigorous methodologies for dealing with missing and uncertain information; improved methods for interpretation of multivariate data sets and for multiobjective decision-making involving trade-offs among conflicting goals; and novel modeling methods as alternatives to traditional mathematical models, for example, agent-based models with appropriate utility functions. More generally, there is a great need to identify and analyze the metrics as the main parameters of sustainability of the system and its effectiveness. Software metrics are quantitative measures of specific attributes of software development, including software process and product. There are several kinds of metrics, based on the analysis of source code, developed during the past few decades for different programming paradigms such as structured programming and object-oriented programming (OOP). An important step in establishing a measurement program is the selection of the measures to use. The selection of the metrics should fit the process used and should have a direct impact on the quality of the delivered software. Different metrics may be appropriate for different products or processes even within the same organization. Metrics validation is another important topic in the area of software measures because their acceptance depends on whether they are able to predict important qualities.

The objectives of this book are:

- To identify existing and easily collectible measures, if possible in the early phases of software development, for predicting and modeling both the traditional attributes of software systems and attributes specifically related to their efficient use of resources, and to create new metrics for such purposes.

- To describe ways to collect these measures during the entire life cycle of a system, using minimally invasive monitoring of design-time processes, and consolidate them into conceptual frameworks to support model building by using a variety of approaches, including statistics, data mining, and computational intelligence.
- To present models and tools to support design-time evolution of systems based on design-time measures and to empirically validate them. The models will support designers by providing suggestions with the idea of realizing an experience factory based on the analysis of the available measures (e.g., by using a model that identifies a vulnerability in the source code and suggests the need for refactoring).

The book is printed by the decision of the Academic Council of Innopolis University. We thank Innopolis University and the Russian Science Foundation (Grant No. 19-19-00623) for supporting us and all the fellow professors and students while writing this book.

Innopolis, Russia   Artem Kruglov
May 2022   Giancarlo Succi

Contents

Chapter 1
Concept and Principles of Measurement

The importance of measurement in research and technology is indisputable. Measurement is the fundamental mechanism of scientific study and development, and it allows to describe the different phenomena of the universe through the exact and general language of mathematics, without which it would be challenging to define practical or theoretical approaches from scientific investigation. Measurement allows us to understand what is happening and why and becomes critical for estimating progress, success, and failures. Indeed, it is very hard (if not impossible) to control what cannot be understood. Moreover, measurement provides great benefits in domains in which it has not been previously widely used or has not been applied at all. The economic, political, and social spheres have started to adopt quantitative methods more often. These aspects of modern society are a challenge to manage. For this purpose, we need data from measurements, the collection and analysis of which by means of smart machines and special tools is becoming more accessible.

1.1 Definitions

Measurement is the process by which numbers or symbols are assigned to attributes of entities in the real world in such a way as to describe them according to clearly defined rules (Fenton et al. 1997).

Example
We need to compare the reliability of software systems. Using the GQM approach (see Sect. 4.2 for more details), the authors provide several software measures (metrics) through questions. The following are the questions and metrics that they

© The Author(s) 2023
A. Kruglov, G. Succi, *Developing Sustainable and Energy-Efficient
Software Systems*, SpringerBriefs in Computer Science,
https://doi.org/10.1007/978-3-031-11658-2_1

selected:[1]

- How likely is the code to have a failure?

    - The number of Modification Requests that are present.
    - The rate at which Modification Requests are issued.
    - The density of Modification Requests over the physical size of the project.

- What is the rate at which failures are detected?

    - The percentage of Modification Requests that are fixed.
    - The speed at which Modification Requests are fixed, when they are fixed.
    - A subjective evaluation of the overall fixing process, performed by analyzing the curve of fixing of Modification Requests.

- What is the rate at which failures are detected?

    - The parameters of the Software Reliability Growth Models.
    - A subjective evaluation of the timings of arrivals of Modification Requests, performed by analyzing the curves of arrivals.

1.2   Meaning and Advantages

Measurement plays an important role throughout all our life in the modern world. But measurement for measurement's sake is not needed. Measurement is one of the steps of research, design, planning, and implementation. Evaluation is essential. Evaluation considers the goals and the context and decides what the concrete measure indicates.

The absence of measurement or weak measurement can lead to the following consequences:

- Lack of measurable targets (Gilb's principle)
  If you do not know what to measure, you cannot improve anything.
- Identification failure
  If you identify your goals or metrics wrongly, your results do not help you to improve; moreover, they can even make your processes worse.
- Lack of quality assurance
  If you cannot measure what you are doing, you cannot ensure quality because you are not capable of controlling the process.

---

[1] Vladimir Ivanov, Alexey Reznik, Giancarlo Succi. Comparing the reliability of software systems: A case study on mobile operating systems.

- Lack of consistent tool evaluation
Your measurement tools need to be consistent (i.e., be capable of independently measuring the same concepts correctly), so that your measurement can be considered reliable.

There are a lot of benefits acquired through measurement. We can categorize them by professional activity.

There are the following advantages for managers:

- Cost
- Productivity
- Quality
- User satisfaction
- Optimization

Indeed, through measurement managers can decrease costs by eliminating useless expenses and increase the productivity of the team and the quality of the produced software, and thus maximize user satisfaction. Optimization of the working process is of utter importance, if you want to succeed.

Also, let us define the advantages for engineers in the following list:

- Requirements testing
- Fault detection
- Meeting goals
- Forecasting

By conducting measurement at the early stages of the development process, engineers can save a lot of time and effort by eliminating useless or invalid requirements and detecting existing and possible faults, thereby sticking to the initial goals.

Moreover, customers, developers, and managers can use software metrics to track the evolution of the project in terms of:

- Hours spent
- Required quality levels
- Requests for new requirements
- Work overtime
- Quality of work

If we talk about the benefits, it is also worth mentioning the following scope of software measurement:

- Cost and effort estimation
Effort is expressed as a function of one or more variables such as the size of the program, the capability of the developers, and the level of reuse. Cost and effort estimation models have been proposed to predict the project cost during the early phases in the software life cycle (e.g., Boehm's COCOMO model, Putnam's slim model, Albrecht's function point model).

- Productivity measures and models
  Productivity can be considered as a function of the value and the cost. Each can be decomposed into different measurable sizes, functionality, time, money, etc.
- Data collection
  The quality of any measurement program is clearly dependent on careful data collection. Data collected can be distilled into simple charts and graphs so that managers can understand the progress and problem of the development. Data collection is also essential for scientific investigation of relationships and trends.
- Quality models and measures
  Quality models have been developed for the measurement of the quality of the product without which productivity is meaningless. These quality models can be combined with productivity models for measuring the correct productivity. These models are usually constructed in a treelike fashion. The upper branches hold important high-level quality factors such as reliability and usability.
- Reliability models
  Most quality models include reliability as a component factor; however, the need to predict and measure reliability has led to a separate specialization in reliability modeling and prediction. The basic problem in reliability theory is to predict when a system will eventually fail.
- Performance evaluation and models
  It includes externally observable system performance characteristics such as response times and completion rates and the internal working of the system such as the efficiency of algorithms. It is another aspect of quality.
- Structural and complexity metrics
  Here we measure the structural attributes of representations of the software, which are available in advance of execution. Then we try to establish empirically predictive theories to support quality assurance, quality control, and quality prediction.
- Capability-maturity assessment
  This model can assess many different attributes of development including the use of tools, standard practices, and more. It is based on the key practices that every good contractor should be using.
- Management by metrics
  Measurement plays a vital role in managing the software project. For checking whether the project is on track, users and developers can rely on the measurement-based chart and graph. The standard set of measurements and reporting methods is especially important when the software is embedded in a product where the customers are not usually well-versed in software terminology.
- Evaluation of methods and tools
  This depends on the experimental design, proper identification of factors likely to affect the outcome, and appropriate measurement of factor attributes.

1.3   Representation Condition

Before defining this condition, one needs to make the following observations.

- A **measurement** is a mapping from the empirical world to the formal, relational world (Fenton et al. 1997).
- A **measure** is the number or symbol assigned to an entity by this mapping in order to characterize an attribute (Fenton et al. 1997).

Representation Condition   A measurement mapping must map entities into numbers and empirical relations into numerical relations that preserve them and vice versa (Fenton et al. 1997).

The measure is **valid** if it satisfies the Representation Condition (Fig. 1.1).

Example
LOC satisfies the Representation Condition for physical application size, but it does not do so for functional application size because one can have a no-so-well-written program with a lot of LOC but with more or less the same functionality and vice versa.

1.4   Measurement Characteristics

Measurement should meet the following characteristics:

- **Sensitivity**
Instrument's ability to accurately measure variability in responses.

  Example

  – A dichotomous response category, such as "agree or disagree," does not allow the recording of subtle attitude changes.

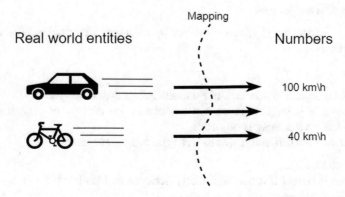

Fig. 1.1   Representation condition. Based on Fenton et al. (1997, p.31)

– A sensitive measure, with numerous items on the scale, may be needed. For instance, increase the number of items (response categories): strongly agree, agree, neutral, disagree, strongly disagree. It will increase a scale's sensitivity.

- **Validity**
  The ability of an instrument to measure what is intended to be measured. Validity of the indicator:

  – Is it a true measure?
  – Are we tapping the concept?

  Example

  – We want to establish how well a programmer did his work. If we choose LOC as a measure of wellness of the programmer's work, will it be a valid measure?

- **Reliability**
  It reflects the degree to which an instrument or scale measures the same way each time it is used under the same condition with the same subjects. Two important dimensions of reliability:

  – **Repeatability**—ability of a measure to remain the same over time despite uncontrolled testing conditions.
  – **Consistency**—indicator of the homogeneity of the items in the measure that tap the construct. In other words, the items should "hang together as a set" and be capable of independently measuring the same concept.

  Example If we run tests several times and every time the results are the same, then we can say that it is a credible measure of reliability of the program.

1.5 Kinds of Metrics

Objective and subjective

A metric is **objective** if it can be taken by an automated device. The metric is **subjective** otherwise.

Examples

- LOC is an objective metric, and Function Points are subjective.
- Measuring how well someone can complete a set number of assignments in a controlled environment is objective.
- Measuring how difficult it was to write the code is subjective.

  Direct and indirect
  A metric is **direct** if it can be directly detected and **indirect** if it is the result of mathematical elaboration on other metrics.

Examples

- LOC, number of errors, duration of testing process, number of defects discovered during test, time a developer spends on a project, and Functional Points are direct.
- Number of errors per LOC (error density) is indirect.

1.6 Measurement Scales

The kind of data received defines the relevant measurement scale. Also, the measurement scale defines the relevant statistical method for analyzing actual data and making conclusions from that data. Each type of measurement scale has a specific use.

A measurement scale is a class of mapping that links empirical and number relations with specific properties.

Each measurement scale should satisfy one or more of the following characteristics:

- Identity—every number on the measurement scale has to be unique.
- Ordered relationship—values should have ordered relationship to one another (magnitude). For example, some values are less and some are more than others.
- Equal intervals—scale units are equal to each other. This characteristic means, for instance, that the difference between 10 and 11 should be equal to the difference between 21 and 22.
- A minimum value of zero—the scale should have a true zero point. There should be no values below this point.

Measurement distinguishes different classes of how to assign symbols to real-world aspects: nominal, ordinal, interval, ratio, and absolute scales.

- **Nominal**
  We use a nominal scale if we create categories and assign real-world entities to these categories. Values attached to variables show a category but do not have an original numerical value. For nominal, any 1:1 mapping is OK.
  Example
  Gender. This is a variable that is measured on a nominal scale. People may be categorized as "female" or "male," but neither value shows less or more "gender" than the other.
- **Ordinal**
  If we can rank the categories of symbols so that we can say that something is higher, larger, smaller, etc., we need an ordinal scale. It satisfies identity and magnitude characteristics. Each value on this scale is unique. Also, ordinal scales show the order of the data according to some criteria. For ordinal, the mapping needs to be strictly increasing.

Example

Answers for the question "How do you rate our product?" in some test—excellent, very good, good, satisfactory, bad, very bad.

- **Interval**

  An ordinal scale is good, but it does not tell us the amount of difference between the categories. Is the difference between excellent and very good the same as between bad and very bad? If we need an answer for this kind of question, we should use an interval scale. An interval scale provides identity, magnitude, and equal interval characteristics. For interval, the mapping must have the form:

  $Y = aX + b$, with $a > 0$

  Example

  The Fahrenheit scale to measure temperature: a difference of 5 degrees between 55 and 60 means the same as 5 degrees between 15 and 20. Through an interval scale, one may know not only the difference between values, like bigger or smaller, but also how much bigger or smaller they are.

- **Ratio**

  Interval scales define the differences between categories. An example is a set of dates. We can either add or subtract two dates, but if we try to multiply or divide two dates, the result will not make any sense. We define a ratio scale as a scale where the mutual proportion between the measurements makes sense. A ratio scale must have a "natural" zero element, that is, an element representing the absence of the property being measured. A ratio scale contains all the above properties, specifically: identity, magnitude, equal intervals, and a minimum value of zero. For ratio, the mapping must have the form:

  $Y = aX$, with $a > 0$

  Example

  The weight of an object, LOC, in a program.

- **Absolute**

  The absolute scale is the most restrictive of all. Absolute measures are counts. The measurement for an absolute scale is made simply by counting the number of elements in the entity set. All arithmetic analysis of the resulting count is meaningful. For absolute, the only acceptable mapping is of the form:

  $Y = X$

  Example

  The number of if statements in a program, the number of failures in a module, etc.

1.7   Software Metrics

Software measurements are of two categories, namely, direct and indirect measures.

Direct measures of the software engineering process include cost and effort applied. Direct measures of the product include lines of code (LOC) produced, execution speed, memory size, and defects reported over a set period of time.

Indirect measures of the product include functionality, quality, complexity, efficiency, reliability, maintainability, and many other "-abilities."

1.7.1 Lines of Code (LOC)

LOC or thousands of LOC (KLOC) has been a very traditional and direct method of metrics of software.

Most traditional measures are used to quantify software complexity. They are simple, easy to count, and very easy to understand. They do not, however, take into account the intelligence content and the layout of the code. These metrics are derived by normalizing the quality and productivity measures by considering the size of the product as a metric.

Size-oriented metrics depend on the programming language used. LOC measures is an older method that was developed when FORTRAN and COBOL programming were very popular. Productivity is defined as KLOC/EFFORT, where effort is measured in person-months. As productivity depends on KLOC, assembly language code will have more productivity, and the more expressive the programming language, the lower the productivity. The LOC method of measurement is not applicable to projects that deal with visual (GUI-based) programming.

It requires that all organizations must use the same method for counting LOC. This is so because some organizations use only executable statements, some use comments, and some do not. So, a standard needs to be established, for instance, using the count of the ";". Once a standard is set, they can be computed automatically (Objective metrics).

Based on the LOC/KLOC count of software, many other metrics can be computed:

- Errors/KLOC
- $/KLOC
- Defects/KLOC
- Pages of documentation/KLOC
- Errors/PM
- Productivity = KLOC/PM (effort is measured in person-months)
- $/Page of documentation

1.7.2 Cyclomatic Complexity

Cyclomatic complexity v(G) was introduced by Thomas McCabe in 1976. It measures the number of linearly independent paths through a program module (Control Flow). The McCabe complexity is one of the more widely accepted software metrics, and it is intended to be independent of language and language format. It is considered as a broad measure of soundness and confidence for a program.

Code complexity correlates with the defect rate and robustness of the application program. Code with good complexity:

- Contains fewer errors
- Is easier and faster to test
- Is easier to understand
- Is easier to maintain

Code complexity metrics are used to locate complex code. To obtain a high-quality software with low cost of testing and maintenance, the code complexity should be measured as early as possible in coding. The developer can adapt their code when recommended values are exceeded.

Recommendations:

- Function length should be 4–40 program lines. A function definition contains at least a prototype, one line of code, and a pair of braces, which makes four lines.
- A function longer than 40 program lines probably implements many functions. (Exception: Functions containing one selection statement with many branches.)
- Decomposing them into smaller functions often decreases readability.
- File length should be 4–400 program lines. The smallest entity that may reasonably occupy a whole source file is a function, and the minimum length of a function is four lines.
- Files longer than 400 program lines (10–40 functions) are usually too long to be understood as a whole.

$v(G)$ could be calculated as:

- Regions in the graph
- Independent paths in the graph
- $E - N + 2$

    where:
    $E =$ number of edges
    $N =$ number of nodes

- $P + 1$

    where:
    $P =$ number of predicated nodes (i.e., if, case, while, for, do)

$v(G) = 1$ for a program consisting of only sequential statements. For a single function, $v(G)$ is one less than the number of conditional branching points in the function. The greater the cyclomatic number, the more execution paths there are through the function, and the harder it is to understand. For dynamic testing, the cyclomatic number $v(G)$ is one of the most important complexity measures, because the cyclomatic number describes the control flow complexity. It is obvious that modules and functions with a high cyclomatic number need more test cases than modules with a lower cyclomatic number. Each function should have at least as many test cases as indicated by its cyclomatic number.

The cyclomatic number of a function should be less than 15. If a function has a cyclomatic number of 15, there are at least 15 (but probably more) execution paths through it. More than 15 paths are hard to identify and test. Functions containing one selection statement with many branches make up an exception. A reasonable upper limit cyclomatic number of a file is 100.

1.7.3   Fan In and Fan Out

The Fan In of a module is the amount of information that "enters" a module. The Fan Out of a module is the amount of information that "exits" a module. We assume all the pieces of information are of the same size. Fan In and Fan Out can be computed for functions, modules, objects, and also non-code components.

Usually parameters passed by values and external variables used before being modified count toward Fan In. External variables modified in the block and returned values count toward Fan Out. Parameters passed by reference depend on their usage.

Structural Fan In (SFIN) and Fan Out (SFOUT) values measure the relationships between files and between procedures. They measure the complexity of the static (design-time) structure of code.

A useful way to look at SFIN and SFOUT is to view them as graph metrics. Visualize procedures (or files) as nodes and calls between them as links. Fan In is the number of links coming into a node. Fan Out is the number of arrows going out of a node.

Fan metrics for files and procedures are related to each other, but they are counted with different rules.

For procedures, structural Fan In and Fan Out are calculated from the procedure call tree:

- SFIN (procedure) = number of procedures that call this procedure
- SFOUT (procedure) = number of procedures this procedure calls

A high SFIN indicates a heavily used procedure, while a low SFIN is the opposite. A high SFOUT means the procedure calls many others. A procedure with SFOUT=0 is a leaf procedure that depends on no other procedures (it may depend on the data it reads, though).

SFIN=0 indicates that no procedure callers were found in the analysis. It does not necessarily indicate a dead procedure, however. The procedure may be in use via an invisible call. An example of this is an event handler which is triggered based on user action. Use the dead code detection feature of Project Analyzer to find and remove dead code.

For files, structural Fan In and Fan Out are calculated from the file dependency tree:

- SFIN (file) = number of files that depend on this file
- SFOUT (file) = number of files this file depends on

A file depends on another file if it requires the other file to compile or run. It may call procedures in the other file, read/write its variables, access its constants, or use its class, interface, UDT, or enum declarations. A high SFIN indicates a heavily used file, while a low SFIN indicates the opposite. A high SFOUT means the file depends on many others. A file with SFOUT=0 is independent of others.

An SFIN value of 2 or more indicates reused code. The higher the fan in, the more reuse.

A high SFIN is desirable for procedures because it indicates a routine that is called from many locations. Thus, it is reused, which is usually a good objective.

A high SFIN is not as desirable for a file. While it can indicate good reuse, it also represents a high level of cross-file coupling. SFIN for a file should be "reasonable." We leave the definition of "reasonable" to be determined case by case.

A special use for procedure-level SFIN is the detection of procedures that could be inlined. If a procedure's SFIN is low but positive, it has a small number of callers. Depending on what the procedure does and how complex it is, you could possibly embed it within the caller(s). This is a speed optimization technique. We do not recommend inlining for usual coding because keeping the code modular improves reuse and legibility.

A high SFOUT denotes strongly coupled code. The code depends on other code and is probably more complex to execute and test.

A low or zero fan out means independent, self-sufficient code. This kind of code is easier to reuse in another project or for another purpose. A file whose SFOUT=0 is a leaf file in the project. You can include it in another project as such and it will most probably continue to work the same way.

To evaluate the average coupling between files, monitor the average SFOUT/file value. This is the average of "how many other files my files depend on." Try to keep this value low. Achieving a low cross-file coupling should be done via restructuring and planning. It should not be achieved by just mechanically joining files—so keep an eye on the file sizes as well. Notice that SFOUT/file is likely to be higher in a large system because the parts of the system need to interact with each other. As your project grows, SFOUT/file is likely to increase even if your code is well designed.

1.7.4   Maintainability Index (MI)

Maintainability Index is calculated with certain formula from LOC, McCabe complexity and Halstead measures. It indicates when it becomes cheaper and/or less risky to rewrite the code instead of changing it.

There are two variants of the Maintainability Index: one that contains comments (MI) and one that does not contain comments (MIwoc). In fact there are three measures:

- MIwoc: Maintainability Index without comments
- MIcw: Maintainability Index comment weight

- MI: Maintainability Index = MIwoc + MIcw

$$MIwoc = 171 - 5.2 * ln(aveV) - 0.23 * aveG - 16.2 * ln(aveLOC),$$

where aveV is average Halstead Volume V per module, aveG is average extended cyclomatic complexity v(G) per module, aveLOC is average count of lines LOCphy per module.

$$MIcw = 50 * sin(\sqrt{2,4} * perCM),$$

where perCM is average percent of lines of comments per module.
  Maintainability Index (MI, with comments) value:

- 85 and above means good maintainability
- 65–85 means moderate maintainability
- <65 means difficult to maintain

  - with really bad pieces of code (big, uncommented, unstructured) the MI value can be even negative.

1.7.5 Quality Metrics

Software metrics can be classified into three categories:

1. Product metrics—These describe the characteristics of the product such as size, complexity, design features, performance, and quality level.
2. Process metrics—These characteristics can be used to improve the development and maintenance activities of the software.
3. Project metrics—These describe the project characteristics and execution.

1.7.5.1 Product Quality Metrics

1. Mean Time to Failure
   This is the time between failures. This metric is mostly used with safety critical systems such as airline traffic control systems, avionics, and weapons.
2. Defect Density
   This measures the defects relative to the software size expressed as lines of code or function point, etc., that is, it measures code quality per unit. This metric is used in many commercial software systems.
3. Customer Problems
   This measures the problems that customers encounter when using the product. It contains the customer's perspective toward the problem space of the software, which includes the non-defect-oriented problems together with the defect problems.
   The problems metric is usually expressed in terms of Problems per User-Month (PUM).

PUM = Total problems that customers reported (true defect and non-defect-oriented problems) for a time period + Total number of license months of the software during the period where Number of license-months of the software = Number of install licenses of the software × Number of months in the calculation period. PUM is usually calculated for each month after the software is released to the market, and also for monthly averages by year.

4. Customer Satisfaction

Customer satisfaction is often measured by customer survey data on a five-point scale from Very dissatisfied to Very satisfied.

Satisfaction with the overall quality of the product and its specific dimensions is usually obtained through various methods of customer surveys. Based on the five-point-scale data, several metrics with slight variations can be constructed and used, depending on the purpose of analysis: percent of completely satisfied customers, percent of satisfied customers, percent of dissatisfied customers, percent of non-satisfied customers.

1.7.5.2 Process Quality Metrics

Based on Lean Six Sigma, there are 13 criteria for process quality:

1. Cp

   Cp is a measure of potential process capability. It is the ratio of the six sigma spread of a process distribution to the tolerance of that distribution. The process must be normally distributed and stable in order to assess Cp. Cp gives the maximum process capability (Cpk) if the process is centered exactly in the middle of the tolerance.

2. Cpk

   Cpk is a measure of the actual process capability. It is calculated by dividing the distance of the process mean to the nearest tolerance limit by 3 standard deviations of the process. Again, the process must be normally distributed and stable before assessing Cpk. See the Statistical Process Control section of the Toolbox for additional help on this subject.

3. First Pass Yield

   Percentage of units that meet specifications without any rework or repair. This is a commonly used measurement but has dubious value for two reasons: (A) rework and repair is often "hidden"—takes place up the line but is not recorded, and (B) multiple defects occurring on a single unit are not captured.

4. Defects Per Unit

   Total number of defects identified on all units divided by the number of units. This metric gives a better measure of quality than First Pass Yield because it captures all the defects. Care must be taken to capture "hidden" rework and repairs that may take place up the line or prior to the reporting point. This metric is also more readily convertible to Defects Per Million Opportunities for Six Sigma projects.

5. Defects Per Million Opportunities (DPMO)

This is a primary Six Sigma metric. Defects per opportunity is used instead of defects per unit to facilitate more direct comparisons between processes with varying levels of complexity. Assembling an automobile is far more complex than manufacturing a patio stone, with far more opportunities for error, so defects per unit is a poor basis for comparing the capability of the manufacturing process.

Defects are a failure of the process to meet a "Critical to Quality Characteristic"—that is to say, a characteristic that customers care about. The number of opportunities must be determined based upon these "Critical to Quality Characteristics" and should be based upon a well-reasoned process. Inflating the number of opportunities will lower the ratio of defects to opportunities and bias the sigma level upward. At the level of three defects per million opportunities, the process is said to have achieved Six Sigma status. An important point to remember when working with DPMO is that customers do not buy opportunities, they buy units. Furthermore, all defects are not created equal, even if they are important to customers. For example, customers care about paint flaws on a car, but they care a lot more about a defect that causes the car not to start. Accordingly, it may be useful to categorize defects into different categories by process and assess the Six Sigma level of each process (e.g., Paint vs. Ignition System).

6. Fill Rate

Percentage of units ordered that are shipped on a given order. If an order for 10 widgets and 10 sprockets is filled, but only 9 of the widgets are shipped due to a product shortage, then the fill rate is 95%.

7. Line Item Fill Rate

Percentage of line items, or SKUs, that are shipped on a given order. If an order for 10 widgets and 10 sprockets is filled, but only 9 of the widgets are shipped due to a product shortage, then the line item fill rate is 50%, because only one of the two line items (SKUs) was shipped 100% complete.

8. Shipment On-Time %

Percent of shipments made on or before the due date.

9. Shipping Errors Per Shipment

Total number of shipping errors (by line item) for a period divided by the number of shipments made during that same period.

10. Warranty Percent of Sales

Warranty dollars paid during a period divided by the net sales for that same period.

11. Warranty Claims per Unit

Total number of warranty claims (not dollars) received during a period divided by the number of units sold during the same period.

12. Survey Complaints (TGWs) per Unit (or per 1000)

The number of complaints, or "Things Gone Wrong," reported on a customer survey divided by the total number of units included in the survey responses. This metric may also be expressed as complaints per 100 units, 1000 units, or even 1,000,000 units.

Table 1.1 Characteristics of invasive and noninvasive measurements

Characteristic	Invasive approach	Noninvasive approach
Collection overhead	High	None
Analysis overhead	High	None
Context switching	Yes	No
Metrics changes	Simple	Tool dependent
Adoption barriers	Overhead, context-switching	Privacy, sensor availability

1.8   Rationale for Noninvasive Measurement

There are two generations in the history of software metrics collection (Johnson et al. 2003). The first iteration employs the Personal Software Process (PSP), a self-improvement method that assists developers in controlling, managing, and improving their workflow (Humphrey 2005). PSP is often known as an "invasive" approach to data collecting since it necessitates direct involvement of participants in the data collection process. The PSP allows users to develop and print a form that logs their effort, size, and defect information. Because the developer must switch the context and manually fill these forms, this approach introduces a lot of overhead due to form filling (Rogers et al. 1995), which uses a lot of resources.

The term "noninvasive" can be used to describe the second generation of software metrics collecting since it signifies that software engineers employ approaches in the development process that do not require their personal engagement in the data collection process (Janes et al. 2014). Table 1.1 (Johnson et al. 2003) depicts the differences between invasive and noninvasive approaches. It is evident that a noninvasive technique decreases the expenses of data gathering and processing, as well as the difficulty of context switching.

A noninvasive collecting system should focus on the following aspects to satisfy the characteristics shown above:

- Automatic collection of product metrics
- Support of the tools that are used by the developers
- Support of the programming language used by the developers
- Automatic installation and update of the tools for data collection

1.9   Conclusion

To assess the quality of the engineered product or system and to better understand the models that are created, some measures are used. These measures are collected throughout the software development life cycle with an intention of improving the software process on a continuous basis. Measurement helps in estimation, quality control, productivity assessment, and project control throughout a software project. Also, measurement is used by software engineers to gain insight into the design and development of work products. In addition, measurement assists in strategic decision-making as a project proceeds.

The cost and effort required to build software, the number of lines of code produced, and other direct measures are relatively easy to collect, as long as specific conventions for measurement are established in advance. However, the quality and functionality of software or its efficiency or maintainability is more difficult to assess and can be measured only indirectly.

We partition the software metrics domain into process, project, and product metrics. We have also noted that product metrics that are private to an individual are often combined to develop project metrics that are public to a software team. Project metrics are then consolidated to create process metrics that are public to the software organization as a whole.

Chapter 2
Metrics of Sustainability and Energy Efficiency of Software Products and Process

Co-authored by Zamira Kholmatova

Software Development Life Cycle (SDLC) is a framework that covers all the stages of software development including requirements elicitating, developing, testing, and maintaining (Ruparelia 2010). Nowadays, for a software system, being sustainable is not enough. For example, the number of applications for mobile devices is constantly growing. In the first quarter of 2022, Android users had about 3.48 million applications to choose from.[1] Having such a great variety of applications, sophisticated users aim at a longer lifespan of batteries. This leads us to the area of energy-efficient computing. However, software quality and reliability as well as the energy efficiency of a system being developed depends on the way of defining and operating software process metrics throughout SDLC. In turn, the efficiency of metrics investigation depends on the software process phases; the early measuring of the software process quality increases the chances of the software being cost-effective and energy-efficient to meet the schedule and the budget (Sultan et al. 2008). However, some of the crucial metrics like complexity of modules or energy consumed on different devices are accessible only during the latter stages. Therefore, the set of measurements through the whole SDLC should be considered to evaluate the software development process quality and efficiency and lead the project to success (Ergasheva et al. 2020). However, the definition of early and late phases varies from one company to another depending on the methodologies used. Consequently, company preferences influence the choice of tools or approaches for assessing and evaluating the quality of the software process or the energy efficiency of the final product. Therefore, the set of measurements to collect for the evaluation or assessment varies as well. This chapter demonstrates the division of SDLC phases into early and late ones, different software quality evaluation methodologies, and a set of measurements.

---

[1] https://www.statista.com/statistics/276623/number-of-apps-available-in-leading-app-stores/.

© The Author(s) 2023
A. Kruglov, G. Succi, *Developing Sustainable and Energy-Efficient Software Systems*, SpringerBriefs in Computer Science, https://doi.org/10.1007/978-3-031-11658-2_2

2.1 Early-Phase Metrics

To monitor the project development, one needs to measure the software process attributes as early as possible. However, before identification of the early-phase metrics, one should define these early phases. During analysis of the literature, we defined a general set of phases and metrics to analyze software quality; these can be metrics of code, design, or the whole system (Ergasheva et al. 2020). Most of the studies consider requirements, design, and seldom code as software life early phases (Ergasheva et al. 2020). However, Davis et al. included User Needs Analysis, Definition of the Solution Space, External Behavior Definition, and Preliminary Design in the early stage of SDLC (Davis 1988). The Requirements Analysis and Definition phase includes feasibility study, requirements elicitation, analysis, validation, and documentation. Moreover, the researchers established the set of stages that SDLC early phases should go through:

- Initial planning phase—constructing the technical and economic basis for the project
- Analysis—defining the requirements for the software configuration
- Design—mapping the requirements to the software components

As was discussed earlier, late defects detection increases the chances of not meeting the budget and time expectations. The cost of removing the defects depends on the time (Phillips et al. 2018). The earlier we define the errors, the fewer financial and time expenses the project will have. For example, errors found in the Acceptance phase are 4–15 times more costly compared to the Design phase, while errors found in the Maintenance phase are 1000 times more costly compared to the Requirements phase (Phillips et al. 2018).

Researchers have noticed that 70% of defects are injected during the early phases while 30% are injected in the late phases (Phillips et al. 2018). There are several studies investigating approaches to assess or evaluate the software quality in the early phases. For example, Aversano et al. investigated the quality of documentation (Aversano et al. 2017). They highlight that the documentation is composed of documents of different kinds including code comments. Therefore, considering design and code phases in the early stages is also important. Many researchers empirically showed the usefulness of metrics collected at a Design or Code phase for defect prediction (Bharathi et al. 2015; Kumar et al. 2017). For example, Basili et al. have shown the effectiveness of five out of the six Chidamber and Kemerer object-oriented metrics to predict class fault-proneness (Basili et al. 1996). Similarly, Kumar et al. suggest using complexity, coupling, and cohesion (CCC) metrics for defect identification (Kumar et al. 2017). Moreover, the Requirements phase highly influences user interest (Davis 1988). However, the activities to be conducted during the early phase depend on the quality assessment and evaluation methods chosen by a company. Many studies were focused on deriving metrics from the following viewpoints (Ergasheva et al. 2020):

- Module complexity
- Module maintainability
- Module functionality

Tables 2.1 and 2.2 show the metrics for the Design and Requirements phases derived from a systematic literature review (Ergasheva et al. 2020). Of the studies found through this SLR 75.7% considered the Requirements and Design phases as early phases of the software development process. Nonetheless, the base metrics are the following: Chidamber and Kemerer's object-oriented metrics, cyclomatic complexity, Lines of Code, and Halstead complexity metric. However, SDLC

Table 2.1 Design phase metrics

Metric	Description
Depth of inheritance tree of a class	The maximum depth of the inheritance graph of each class
Number of children of a class	The number of direct descendants for each class
The number of direct descendants for each class	The number of classes to which a given class is coupled
Response for a class	The number of methods that can potentially be executed in response to a message received by an object of that class
Weighted methods per class	The complexity of an individual class
Lack of cohesion on methods	The number of pairs of member functions without share instance variables, minus the number of pairs of member functions with shared instance variables
Edge count	The number of edges found in a given module control from one module to another
Node count	The number of nodes found in a given module
Branch count	Branch count metrics
Call pairs	The number of calls to other functions in a module
Condition count	The number of conditionals in a given module
Cyclomatic complexity	The cyclomatic complexity of a module
Software progress metric	Simple top-level measure of progress in completing the design, code, and integration phases
Defect density	Requires tracking defect reports against the size of the software (in lines of code, non-comment source statements, or functional points)
Size of modules	Size of each module (in non-comment source statements/ functional points)
Software complexity	The cyclomatic complexity, data flow complexity, and system design complexity
Experience of design and development team	Measures the relevant design and development experience, motivation, programmer capability during the design and development phase of SDLC

Table 2.2 Requirements phase metrics

Metric	Description
Requirements traceability	The portion of the requirements has been allocated to the software requirements documents and then translated into the design, coded, and tested
Requirements definition	The portion of the software requirements is defined satisfactorily (unambiguous, testable, and acceptable to the user)
Requirements stability	The number of units or modules affected by change requests compared to the total number
Requirement fault density	The fraction of faulty requirements specification documents
Actual requirement	Total number of initial requirements present in the project
Volatile requirements	Total number of requirements change requests (insert/delete/update) made during the project cycle
Requirement schedule	Total number of days (estimated) required to complete the task

software metrics are usually uncertain. The uncertainty, vagueness, and imprecision in software metrics can be captured by fuzzy set theory (Yadav et al. 2013).

2.2   Late-Phase Metrics

Almost all the studies investigating the whole SDLC separate the late phase into Development, Testing, and Deployment.

There are two different approaches to the development phase quality evaluation: static analysis and dynamic analysis. Static analysis requires analysis of the code with the help of additional tools while dynamic analysis requires human intervention in the code analysis. Software fault prediction helps to improve the quality of software during the development phase (Kumar et al. 2016). However, one needs to run different kinds of tests after changes to be sure that the integration was successful. But rerunning tests each time increases the time, cost, and resources spent on a project. Some researchers suggested approaches for prioritizing and selecting test cases based on relevant data from experiments or using specialized algorithms (Bajaj et al. 2019; Silva et al. 2016), while another study introduced a framework for test execution and test review phase quality metrics evaluation (Machado et al. 2016).

Development phase metrics are the most popular measurements defined in existing publications. For example, Hota et al. (2019) have shown the set of code metrics affecting the source code. The researchers showed that coupling metrics achieve better performance than such metrics as size, cohesion, and inheritance. Nevertheless, it is important to investigate the test metrics while considering the quality of the software. The Test phase metrics are based on test cases prioritization steps (Silva et al. 2016):

- Inferring the relevance of classes requires the following set of metrics:
  - Features relevance
  - Correlations among features and classes
  - Class relevance
- Calculating class criticality:
  - Coupling
  - Complexity
  - Relevance
- Test criticality computation

Despite the Deployment phase being a critical stage of SDLC nowadays, only the minor publications are dedicated to the Deployment phase metrics. As a result, Tables 2.3, 2.4, and 2.5 show the metrics related to the Development, Testing, and Deployment phases.

Table 2.3 Development phase metrics

Metric	Description
NLOC	Number of lines of code. This is calculated as the number of new-line characters per file (and function)
TCOMM	Total number of comments
CohM	Cohesion metric
DIT	Depth of inheritance tree of a class
CBO	Coupling between objects
LCOM	Lack of cohesion in methods
NOC	Number of children
DEP_ON_CHILD	Dependence on a descendant
FAN_IN	Count of calls by higher modules
RFC	Response for class
VMC	Weighted methods per class
CC	Measures the number of linearly independent paths through a program's source code
ev(G)	Essential complexity: measures the extent to which a flow graph can be reduced by decomposing all the subflow graphs
iv(G)	Design complexity: cyclomatic complexity of a module's reduced flow graph
Defect density	Number of defects per lines of code
Parameter count	The number of parameters a function takes
Code change interval	High frequency of check-ins might imply a lot of modifications leading to an increase in defect probability

Table 2.4 Testing phase metrics

Metric	Description
Defect modification	The number of identified modifications for each defect per function
TNT	Total number of test cases
NFT	Number of failed test cases
NPT	Number of passed test cases
NET	Number of empty test cases
NPAT	Number of passed acceptance tests
Open defects	Number of open defects

Table 2.5 Deployment phase metrics

Metric	Description
Throughput	The total amount of work delivered in a certain time period
System performance	Accuracy, efficiency, and speed of executing computer program instructions
Mean Time To Failure (MTTF)	Maintenance metric that measures the average amount of time a non-repairable asset operates before it fails
Mean Time Before Failure (MTBF)	Predicted elapsed time between inherent failures of a mechanical or electronic system, during normal system operation

The metrics presented in Tables 2.3, 2.4, and 2.5 can be tracked with DevOps tools. One of the most popular DevOps tools nowadays is SonarQube (Guaman et al. 2017). Several researchers investigated existing tools like SonarQube to assess the metrics in the code (Guaman et al. 2017). They evaluated technical debt as an indicator of quality attributes like security, changeability, reliability, and testability. SonarQube can help developers understand how not to increase the technical debt.

The late phases evaluation is different from the early phases. The late phases require separate systems such as Jenkins or SonarQube to check the quality (Armenise 2015).

With the increased demand for high-quality software and its continuous integration, it is important to track software quality and monitor the software development process. We addressed the important aspects of the early and late phases of the SDLC and the existing software quality models together with the DevOps tools to track software process quality metrics during the whole SDLC.

2.3 Metrics of Energy Consumption

With the high demand for information technologies, the problem of energy consumption became a vital problem. One of the ways to address this concern is to control the energy spent by a software. For example, a group of researchers showed that refactoring the code smells reduces energy consumption by up to 87% (Palomba et al. 2019). Moreover, it was found that choosing the wrong collections type in Java language can increase the energy spent by a software by up to 300%.

Ergasheva et al. (2020) systematized metrics of energy consumption in software systems through a systematic literature review. They classified the metrics found into the following categories:

- Hard metrics, which can be found through physical measurement
- Code metrics, which can be analyzed using code
- Runtime metrics, which are related to the dynamic analysis of applications
- Indirect metrics, which refer to the specific energy models
- Process metrics, which can be assessed through the analysis of the software development process
- Others, which are mostly related to the specific system's operations

Since we are interested in software metrics that can be assessed throughout the whole SDLC without dependency on any specific energy consumption models, we can focus on code and process metrics. Table 2.6 shows an example of such metrics that are used to evaluate the energy spent by a software (Ergasheva et al. 2020). Moreover, there already exist tools to derive these metrics like MEMT (Liu et al. 2020), PETrA (Di Nucci et al. 2017), PUPiL (Zhang et al. 2016), and many others.

Table 2.6 Metrics for assessing energy consumption

Metric	Description
Lines of code	Number of lines of code
Number of invocations	The number of executions of a program or function
Cyclomatic complexity	The number of flows through a piece of code
Number of defects per unit size	The number of defects found per unit size of a product
Depth of inheritance tree	The distance from class Object in the inheritance hierarchy
Life cycle cost metrics	Relation between efforts needed for redesigning an application for energy consumption optimization and the potential energy savings
Number of static attributes	The number of methods whose signatures differ is known as overloading

2.4   Conclusion

As one can notice, a project's success requires monitoring and analysis of the software development process throughout the whole SDLC. To meet the time and cost expectations, one should keep tracking software engineering metrics as early as possible. Early phases of SDLC include requirements management, design, and sometimes code phases. However, not all the important factors can be monitored during this period. Therefore, the late phase metrics should also be involved. The late phases usually consist of development, testing, and deployment.

Nowadays, the efficiency of a software in terms of consumed energy also impacts the quality of the overall project. To create energy-efficient solutions, developers have to track the energy consumption during the software development process. From the tables given within this chapter, we can notice that there is still no overall framework for tracking both software quality and energy consumption. One of the main reasons for this is that such analysis requires the participation of developers, which increases time costs. Therefore, as an alternative, we can suggest using the noninvasive systems to model the energy consumption of systems being developed.

Chapter 3
System Energy Consumption Measurement

Co-authored by Gcinizwe Dlamini

This chapter describes the theory and practical implementation of estimating the power consumption of computer devices. Different energy consumption estimation and monitoring approaches are discussed. The evolution of the methods and devices used to measure energy consumed by computer devices and their components is discussed. The challenges faced by the research community in measuring and monitoring energy consumption at different stages of software development are presented. Lastly a machine learning-based approach used for estimating energy consumption in a computer system running on a Windows or Linux operating system is presented. The proposed approach tries to address some of the challenges faced by the software development and research community in data retrieval and estimation of energy consumption in a system. The approach uses information about memory, CPU, and RAM utilization metrics to estimate the overall energy consumption.

3.1 Introduction

Over the years, the task to reduce energy consumed by a system has been mainly assigned to computer hardware developers. This is mainly because it is believed that the hardware is the principal component that consumes more electrical energy. However, the software also plays a vital role in power usage. Hardware works hand in hand with software programs. Gradually over recent years software engineers have been putting more effort in developing green software. As evidence has been presented over the years, it has become clear that computers and other IT infrastructure consume significant amounts of electricity, placing a heavy burden on our electric grids and contributing to greenhouse gas emissions. For this reason, the field of green software engineering has emerged.

© The Author(s) 2023
A. Kruglov, G. Succi, *Developing Sustainable and Energy-Efficient Software Systems*, SpringerBriefs in Computer Science, https://doi.org/10.1007/978-3-031-11658-2_3

Green software engineering is concerned more about climate science, software architecture and practices, electronic devices power consumption, hardware, and data center design. The main question for green software engineers is about the greenness of software and hardware under development. Green software encompass three main phases of the software life cycle: (1) software usage, (2) software design, and (3) software implementation. The main goal is to reduce the amount of energy utilized in each of the phases and have minimal negative impact on the environment.

The first step toward designing green AI and software is measuring the energy consumption and pinpointing the different software components that increase the energy consumption (i.e., abnormal behavior recognition). The second step is recommending ways that could help increase the greenness of the system without tampering with the software's overall quality or performance (i.e., accuracy). It is worth noting that the measurement and recommendation are to be scalable and automated. The first step is addressed in this chapter.

Measuring the energy consumed by a computer system is a challenging task. The challenge is not only because of the fast-increasing advancements in technology but because of the different levels of granularity at which the energy can be measured and the introduction of cloud computing services. Cloud computing has increased the complexity of estimating the greenness of a software product at different phases (i.e., implementation and usage). In a very simple and basic case, hardware power meters are the solution for measuring the overall energy consumed by a physical computer system since they can provide readings about the energy consumption instantly. However, this approach does not help in pinpointing the computer components that need optimization because of high energy consumption.

Over the years, researchers have proposed different approaches which are alternatives to power meters and to measure energy consumption at different levels of granularity during the software development process (i.e., Alsultanny 2018; Bekaroo et al. 2016; Conti et al. 2016a; Mahesri et al. 2004). Among the proposed approaches machine learning-based approaches have been one of the most outstanding. Machine learning (ML) has found its way into many domains and has been outperforming traditional solutions to problems in different life applications including health-care systems (Chen et al. 2017), cyber security (Kabir et al. 2018), manufacturing (Martı̇ et al. 2015), fraud detection (Zhang et al. 2018b), software quality assurance (Sidhu et al. 2022), and numerous other fields (Chandola et al. 2009). In this chapter, the ML-based approach is presented as another better, cheaper, and simple approach to measure energy consumed by a computer system in the software development process.

3.2 Energy Measurements Methods

Over the years, researchers and engineers have developed hardware and software tools to measure power consumption. Figure 3.1 presents a taxonomy of these developed tools and software for power consumption measurement.

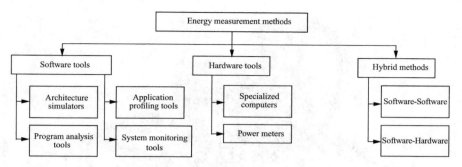

Fig. 3.1 Energy measurement methods taxonomy

3.2.1   Hardware Tools

Physical power monitors are the most accurate tools to measure the energy consumed by any device connected to an electric socket. Power monitors are directly connected to the power source of the device and measure the actual power leveraged at any instant of time. Despite the precision of the approach to measure the energy consumed by a system, it becomes unfeasible when scaled up. In addition to inability to scale, power meters can be challenging to set up (i.e., when measuring the energy consumed by a smartphone). An example of a power monitor can be seen in Fig. 3.2 taken from[1] with modifications. Figure 3.3 presents a general approach to measure the energy consumed by a system as it executes a specific set of instructions. As a result, most power monitors over the years have been integrated to software of a specific hardware which is believed to be the main source of energy consumption (i.e., CPU).

In a computer system, the CPU and processors are one of the main components that consume more energy. Intel, one of the giant computer chip developers, developed an energy measuring and monitoring tool called Intel Power Gadget. Intel Power Gadget (McKay et al. 2019) is an energy monitoring tool for Intel processors. It supports Windows and macOS. Intel Power Gadget provides callable APIs to get energy consumption information from code. In one of the latest updates, multi-socket system support was added. This has served as a first step toward awareness on the amount of energy consumed by a computer system as a whole. The awareness is not only dedicated to system administrators but also to software developers/programmers. Programmers can develop software knowing how much energy it is going to consume as it spends more time utilizing the CPU.

Intel is not the only computer hardware manufacturer to have made efforts in developing tools that measure and monitor energy consumed by hardware such as the CPU. Microsoft developed a tool called Joulemeter (Joulemeter 2010).

---

[1] https://www.fluke.com/en-us/product/condition-monitoring/power/3540-power-monitor-sensor.

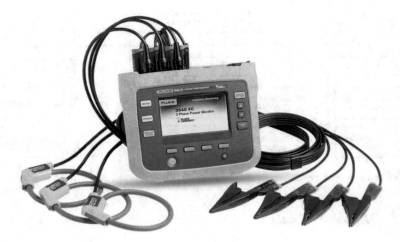

Fig. 3.2   Power monitor

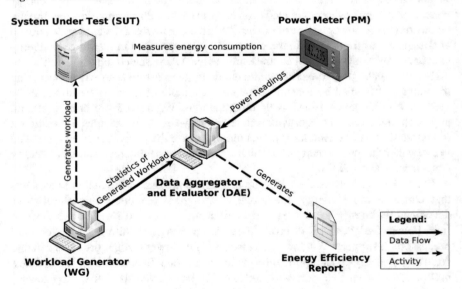

Fig. 3.3   Power usage and hardware utilization of software

Joulemeter (Goraczko 2010) is no longer available for public download. Joulemeter estimates the energy consumption of various computer hardware components such as CPU and I/O devices. This tool is less accurate when compared to a physical power meter such as the one presented in Fig. 3.2. One of the main features of Joulemeter is that it distinguishes system energy, software energy, and VM energy. Nvidia, one of the leading video card producers, has developed a tool that measures and monitors the energy consumed by the graphics processing unit (GPU) hardware.

3.2.2   *Software Tools*

Software tools include software programs that estimate the system components' or the whole system energy consumption. Usually the estimation of energy consumed by a system is based on the system profile and the workload. Most approaches use mathematical models as bases for energy consumption. Over the years, researchers have developed mathematical models that determine the absolute level of power, which is necessary to transfer 1 Bit of Random Access Memory (RAM) from 0 to 1. Figure 3.4 presents a simple example of how the majority of software tools estimate energy consumption based on mathematical models.

The RAM is one of the power-sensitive components of a computer system. The developed mathematical models work hand in hand with energy-efficient hardware developers. The mathematical models are used to evaluate the greenness

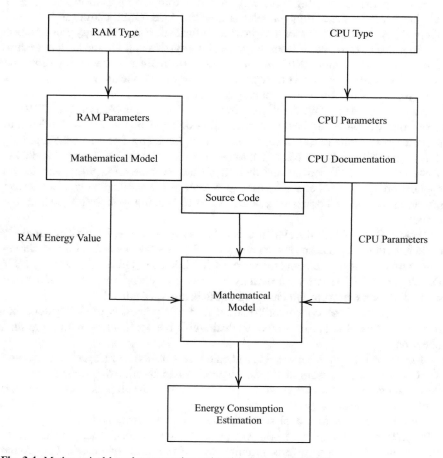

Fig. 3.4 Mathematical-based consumption estimation approach for CPU

of developed hardware before being deployed into production. Multiple software tools to estimate energy consumption have been developed over the years, and some of them are operating system specific.

One of the tools dedicated to estimate energy consumption on Linux operating systems is called PowerTop (PowerTop n.d.). PowerTop is an open-source Linux tool for diagnosing issues with power consumption of computers. The main features of PowerTop are visualizing and presenting information about the energy consumed by each process running in the system. One drawback of PowerTop is that it relies on other external measurements of power.

Similar to PowerTop, McPAT (Li et al. 2009) is a framework for designing a processor. The main difference when compared to PowerTop is that it can model multicore and many core processors with a comprehensive structure. McPAT models not only performance metrics, but also energy metrics, based on analytical power models.

Most energy monitoring tools rely on data from the app/process while it is running. Usually, the main parameter is the CPU load. Often it runs as a service. pTop (Do et al. 2009) is a tool that provides information about energy consumption for the process. It uses data from the parts of the system that use the largest amount of energy: CPU, memory, NIC, and disk. One of the main advantages of pTop is the possibility to help developers create energy-optimized applications, and it provides energy-aware application programming interfaces.

Nadine Amsel and Bill Tomlinson created Green tracker (Amsel et al. 2010)— a tool that estimates the energy consumption of applications that is divided into groups. Users define groups themselves. At first, Green tracker uses benchmarking tests to get CPU statistics. Next, it saves information about time, process, and CPU usage at intervals; based on this data, it creates average CPU utilization for an application. Green tracker can be used to determine the application with the lowest power consumption. For example, Firefox 3.0.10 is better than Safari 4.0.3 in that aspect.

Brown et al. (2006) developed a battery life measurement toolkit for making reliable battery life measurements on Linux. This toolkit consists of a test framework and a number of example workloads (Idle, Reader, Office, DVD Player, SW Developer, and 3D-Gamer). The battery life measurement approach here uses a wall clock measurement from full charge until the battery is depleted.

Tools of this type collect information from all processes of the system, but because of this, it is hard for them to distinguish the applications with more than one process.

Tools of this group are created based on the power model of a specific processor. They count energy consumption for each processor instruction or group of processor instructions. This information can be used by software developers to optimize their application's power usage.

The first attempt to model such a power cost was described by Tiwari et al. (1994). The authors evaluated the energy cost of every instruction and took into account inter-instruction effects: circuit state, stalls, and cache misses. They found the base cost by looping in one instruction. Then researchers used a similar approach to sequences of instruction to obtain information about the circuit state effect. The next step was the experimental determination of the cost of the stall and the cache miss. In the end, they united all their results and created a framework that can estimate the energy consumption of a program.

Tiwari et al. (1996) continued to study this field and described two techniques for measurements: Board-Based Measurements and Tester-Based Measurements. They repeated the previous approach to three new processors and came up with the following observations: memory access is much more expensive than registry access, reordering instructions can reduce power consumption, each processor has its features, and developers can use them to create energy-efficient software.

Mazouz et al. (2017) presented a method that corresponds to both architecture simulators and program analysis groups, and its purpose is to estimate the energy consumption of multicore processors. The resulting energy is the sum of static and dynamic power. The static power is the power of core and uncore components: AlU, L1, L2, L3 cache, etc. Dynamic power is the energy consumed by instructions. Therefore, this method can help developers to correlate code and power usage.

Conti et al. (2016b) developed MTPlug, the framework for identifying laptop users from their energy traces. The framework is based on machine learning models for data preprocessing, segmentation, and feature extraction; however, the raw data comes from specific wall-socket smartmeters, which significantly reduce the practical implementation of this approach.

Li et al. (2003) proposed a method for estimating OS runtime energy consumption. The routine-level OS power model is a model where the average power of OS routines is known, and if we measure the execution time for each routine, then we can compute overall energy consumption.

3.2.3 Hybrid Tools

Hybrid methods create a collaboration between more than one measurement method (i.e., both software tools and hardware power meters). Such a collaboration assists to obtain more precise power readings that can be associated with software components.

e-Surgeon is a composition of PowerAPI and Jalen at a finer grain. Power consumption in e-Surgeon is estimated based on the program's methods and real-time execution. e-Surgeon collects information regarding CPU performance counters (e.g., time and network traffic) through both the operating system (via PowerAPI) and bytecode instrumentation or statistical sampling (via Jalen). e-Surgeon aggregates energy consumption collected by PowerAPI for multiple processes into one result.

PowerScope maintains a digital multimeter to profile and sample software energy consumption. Such a multimeter is controlled by another computer that collects all power readings. PowerScope maps energy consumption to the program structure and procedures. Power readings are collected at runtime but not analyzed until the program terminates. PowerScope is free of any profiling overhead since it performs a statistical sampling of the power consumption and the system activity over the collected measurements.

3.3   The Challenges of Estimating the Consumed Energy in Software Development

As the number of connected devices increases year by year worldwide, evaluating the energy efficiency of each device is becoming an ever more important and critical task. Understanding the energy fingerprint of computer devices is a step toward green IT and saving the planet. Being aware of the greenness of a software mainly in the software development domain contributes to designing energy-efficient software. The amount of energy consumed while developing a software product can be measured at different levels of granularity and software development. Measuring energy cost for developing a software product at different levels of granularity does not come at a low cost in terms of complexity.

Measuring energy consumed by any electrical appliance has been a challenging and complicated task on its own. The estimation and monitoring get more complicated when it comes to measuring the energy consumption of different components of a connection to other computers or devices. Understanding the root of the challenges is key in designing a framework to monitor and measure energy consumption in the software domain.

The first challenge is related to the metric that are is measured: power, which is a variable sinusoidal voltage. Accurately measuring the amount of energy consumed by a computer device is complex since most computer devices by their nature operate in a pulse signal mode when the current is not sinusoidal. The second problem is related to the accurate collection of energy consumption metrics in a noninvasive manner. Without the input of the device specifications, it is nearly impossible for the mathematical models (as presented in Fig. 3.4) to estimate the overall energy consumption. The third challenge is related to the advancements in technology and ever-increasing number of connected devices (IoT). In a case where part of the software uses cloud services, it is nearly impossible to measure the energy consumed by the cloud computing service such as the server. So calculating the exact amount of energy consumed by the software product that is under development gets more complex.

3.4   Machine Learning-Based Approach for Energy Consumption Measurement

This section presents a case study that proposes a machine learning (ML)-based approach to estimate the energy consumed by a system based on utilization of system core devices such as CPU, RAM, and virtual memory. In addition to the ML approach, it presents a use case of a noninvasive data collection framework.

3.4.1   Methodology

The proposed methodology for estimating energy consumed by a system in a noninvasive manner is presented in Fig. 3.5. This approach is based on machine learning and is implemented based on a framework called Innometrics. Details about each machine learning approach are presented in the following subsections.

3.4.2   Data Collection

The data collection and labeling task is one of the most challenging tasks in machine learning. Based on the nature of the problem that is to be solved in energy consumption estimation and monitoring, it is highly recommended that the approach be noninvasive and accurate. Innometrics (Ciancarini et al. 2020) provides the noninvasive feature of the proposed approach. Innometrics is available for three main operating systems (i.e., Windows, Mac OS, and Linux) in terms of data collectors deployed on the user devices. The data collectors retrieve data related to general information about the processes executed on the machine and extract their resource utilization such as CPU, RAM, and disk usage. For energy consumption monitoring purposes of the data about the resource utilization by each process, the data is sampled continuously in a uniform manner.

3.4.3   Data Preprocessing

Curating the data before learning the underlying data patterns is essential and crucial. To preprocess the data before parsing it to the machine learning model, we performed a couple of steps. Firstly, we removed all records with missing values. Secondly, the data records were aggregated according to the capture time using summation. We refrain from data scaling and data normalization since they do not make any significant impact on tree-based model performance. For feature selection, three features were selected to be used as model input, namely: (1) ratio of the process's resident set size to the physical memory on the machine, (2) virtual memory size of a process (vram), and (3) the central processing unit (CPU) utilization of a process. All the selected features are numerical.

3.4.4   Machine Learning Models

The proposed machine learning model here is an ensemble learning-based algorithm called CatBoost (Dorogush et al. 2018). The ML method was proposed and developed by Yandex researchers. CatBoost is an ensemble learning algorithm

Table 3.1 The ML model optimal hyper-parameters

Parameter	Windows OS	Linux OS	Windows & Linux
# of iterations	500	2000	2000
Learning rate	0.03	0.1	0.1
loss_function	RMSE	RMSE	RMSE
depth	4	4	4
l2_leaf_reg	7	5	5
eval_metric	RMSE	RMSE	RMSE

which is based on decision trees. The model hyper-parameters were tuned. The ability of the model to be trained on accelerated hardware such as a graphics processing unit (GPU) made it easy to conduct a hyper-parameters search. The optimal hyper-parameters are presented in Table 3.1.

3.4.5 Performance Evaluation

After a machine learning model is trained to recognize underlying data patterns and estimate the target (i.e., energy consumed by a system) given an input, it is important to evaluate the performance. To evaluate the ML model, three popular standard metrics are used: mean squared error (MSE), mean absolute error (MAE), and coefficient of determination (R^2). The calculation of the metrics is as follows:

$$MSE = \frac{1}{n} \sum_{t=1}^{n} \left(y_i - \hat{y}_i\right)^2 \tag{3.1}$$

$$MAE = \left(\frac{1}{n}\right) \sum_{i=1}^{n} \left|y_i - \hat{y}_i\right| \tag{3.2}$$

$$R^2 = 1 - \frac{\sum_{t=1}^{n} \left(y_i - \hat{y}_i\right)^2}{\sum_{t=1}^{n} \left(y_i - \bar{y}_i\right)^2} \tag{3.3}$$

where $\hat{y}$ is the predicted value, n is the total number of data samples, and $\bar{y}$ is the mean value of y calculated by $\frac{1}{n} \sum_{i=1}^{n} y_i$.

3.4.6   Experimental Results (Tables 3.2, 3.3, and 3.4)

Table 3.2 Train data distribution

Operating system	Number of samples	Period	Missing values	Duplicate rows
Linux	158 327	1 month	0	77 721
Windows	62 342	2 days	6	36 584
Total	220 669	33 days	6	114 305

Table 3.3 Test data distribution

Operating system	Number of samples	Period	Missing values	Duplicate rows
Linux	160 128	24 days	0	78 658
Windows	91 294	2 days	8	50 825
Total	251 422	26	8	129 483

Table 3.4 Performance measures

Metric	Windows OS	Linux OS	Windows & Linux
MSE	2e-06	0.00175638	0.000671
MAE	0.000418	0.0288128	0.010409
R^2	-1.081685	0.91098569	0.921411

3.5   Conclusion

The presented results provide a starting point for the research community as it tries to accurately estimate the amount of energy consumed in software development leveraging the benefits of ML. However, there is still room for improvement in the proposed approach above. The challenges faced by the research community have been presented and the existing energy consumption measurement tools have also been discussed.

Chapter 4
GQM and Recommender System for Relevant Metrics

Co-authored by Anna Gorb

Measurement in software development has its own specific challenges. The developer may easily try to count all the lines of code of the program. Yet, that will not give an answer about the quality of the code, as it is much more complex and includes many other aspects beyond the lines of code. In order to understand the effects of actions that are implemented in software development and gain an understanding of how improvements can be made for future software development processes, a certain purpose should be added to the measurement process. This can be reached with the use of the GQM model that allows to select goal-focused metrics among all possible variants. However, even after the application of the GQM model, too many metrics may remain, which will affect the efficiency of the processes and their collection and interpretation will not benefit the project. With the use of the recommender system, it is possible to choose the most useful among them without any wastage of resource.

4.1 Introduction

Software engineering is a unique phenomenon, standing so close to formal and rigorous mathematics, and at the same time to art, that it is impossible to define or frame. Software tasks have no standard algorithmic solutions, and it is very difficult to formalize the quality degree of the final product. That is why, as noted earlier in this book, every software project needs properly chosen metrics. They help to evaluate the processes, products, and resources in the early stages of the development and shape the right direction accordingly.

However, there are several problems to consider when choosing metrics. Firstly, they need to be selected very carefully and competently, as incorrectly defined metrics can lead the project away from its goal and drain valuable time and resources

© The Author(s) 2023
A. Kruglov, G. Succi, *Developing Sustainable and Energy-Efficient Software Systems*, SpringerBriefs in Computer Science,
https://doi.org/10.1007/978-3-031-11658-2_4

allocated to the project. The second problem is that there exist an infinite number
of metrics and ways to categorize them. Overloading in their number can lead to a
shift in priorities and loss of focus on the project.

4.2   Concept of Goal-Question-Metric

Because the problem of metrics selection is so important and complex, usually the
development team hires a specialist who goes through a long a list of requirements
and just as long a list of metrics and allocates a basic scope of metrics for further
use. However, this is costly both financially and in terms of time. Consequently,
several structured and formal approaches to derive metrics have emerged to simplify
this process. Among them, the most widely known in the scientific area is the
Goal-Question-Metric model, invented by Victor Basili and David Weiss. With this
technology, it is possible to solve the first problem mentioned in the Introduction—
exclude the possibility of deviations from the project goals with the inappropriate
metrics.

   GQM, according to Basili et al. (1994), stands for "goal, question, metric" and
allows one to define the goals to achieve by clarifying the questions on how the
goal can be reached with the collected data. For that purpose, GQM defines a
measurement model on three levels:

1. **Goal**—The goal for which all the work is done, all the artifacts and processes
   being produced.
2. **Question**—Several questions defined based on the goal to outline a way to
   achieve it.
3. **Metric**—A set of metrics that answer a given question in a measurable way.

   The GQM model can be represented in the form of a tree, the root of which is the
goal. The branches of the tree are represented by questions that allow the goal to be
made more specific. And the leaves are the metrics, the measurable outcome of the
whole model (Fig. 4.1).

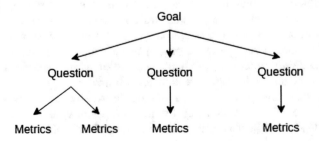

Fig. 4.1 Hierarchical structure of the GQM model

Defining the GQM model, namely, questions and metrics, helps to determine why and how it is possible to achieve the goal. Consequently, the movement from the root of the tree to the leaves-metrics makes the abstraction itself more understandable.

4.3   The Goal-Question-Metric Process

According to Solingen et al. (1999), there emerged certain goal-setting methodological processes that include the GQM model construction:

1. **Planning phase**—The first step for the project selection, initial artifacts creation, and planning.
2. **Definition phase**—The GQM model construction and documentation.
3. **Data Collection phase**—Collect data according to the defined GQM.
4. **Interpretation phase**—Interpret the collected data regarding the defined metrics, which will give the answers to the stated questions. With the gathered results, the achievement of the goal can be evaluated.

In the first phase, the team prepares the ground for further steps by identifying the project area, its clients, and their needs and by the creation of the initial documentation.

All of the management, training involvement, and project planning are done during this phase. After the plan is made, the *definition phase* starts. During the *definition phase*, the GQM deliverable is developed, and the information for the deliverable is acquired from informative sources such as interviews, analysis, and articles. The *data collection phase* presumes the measurement itself. During the data collection phase, the data is gathered, stored, and defined. Then the *interpretation phase* begins when the measurements are used to answer the stated questions, and the answers are further used for the stated goals (Fig. 4.2).

For more details, the steps of the GQM method are:

1. **Develop business goals**—Develop a set of corporate, division, and project business goals and associated measurement goals for productivity and quality.

Fig. 4.2 Four phases of the Goal-Question-Metric method

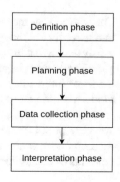

In other words, aims that should be reached or investigated should be stated at this step in such a way that will easily allow questions to be found that should define the goals. Usually, the goal is specifying the purpose of measurement, object to be measured, issue to be measured, and viewpoint from which the measure is taken. For instance, the goal can be stated as "Improve (a purpose) the timeliness (a quality issue) of change request processing (a process) from the project manager's point of view (obviously, viewpoint)."

2. **Generate questions**—Generate questions (based on models) that define those goals as completely as possible in a quantifiable way. Questions usually break down the goal into its major components. They should also be specific enough in order to be refined into metrics on the next step. An example of a question for the goal stated previously is "What is the current change request processing speed?"

3. **Specify the measures**—Specify the measures needed to be collected to answer those questions and track process and product conformance to the goals. It should also be noted that any metric can help to answer more than one question, that is, it can be used two or more times. Examples of metrics for the question above are "Average cycle time" and "Percentage of cases outside of the upper time limit."

4. **Define mechanisms for data collection**—Choose the best-fit mechanisms that will help collect necessary data. They can range from invasive methods when somebody can even pause processes in order to capture some metrics to noninvasive when the processes are observed from outside without any intervention. For example, considered metrics can be collected by analyzing log files produced by the system.

5. **Collect, validate, and analyze the data**—Process the data in real time to provide feedback to projects in order to correct or improve the process. This step often includes processing of collected data with the usage of methods and tools provided by statistics and probability theory.

All this helps to make sure that the selected metrics are aligned to the goal and will guide the project in the right direction.

4.4 Recommender Systems

The solution for the second issue can become the recommender system. Automation in our century is the main engine of progress. That is why recommendation systems were created to automate our choices. In order for users not to have to search through a multitude of options that do not interest them, the recommender systems choose the most interesting ones for them instead. This mechanism is extremely useful in modern online stores, such as Amazon, content generators such as YouTube, and search engines like Google. It can be seen that all the platforms from these examples are very popular and have a large user base. This is one of the main features of recommender systems. With a large number of users, services can collect huge amounts of data, which can be analyzed to develop recommender systems. Collected datasets can consist of any information that the computer can process—text data, numbers, boolean values, and much more.

Because of their widespread use in different fields, many types of recommender algorithms have appeared over time. The first and best known of them is collaborative filtering (Schafer et al. 2007). There are several types of collaborative filtering algorithms. User-based filtering finds the most similar users based on an analysis of their preferences and makes recommendations based on that comparison (Wang et al. 2021). The item-based method, on the other hand, is based on item analysis. This approach compares item ratings with one another and produces a result based on similarity (Sarwar et al. 2001). In general, collaborative filtering is effective for solving problems that do not have a detailed list of characteristics for each item. However, it also has its disadvantages. For example, it is not possible to make a good recommendation if there are no similar users or similar rated items. One should also keep in mind that the higher the amount of data, the better this method will work, but the longer the algorithm will take to work (Isinkaye et al. 2015).

In order to generate recommendations when there are detailed descriptions of items but not a lot of collected data, the second type of recommender algorithm—content-based filtering—was invented (Pazzani et al. 2007). As the name suggests, the focus is shifted from the user to the recommended product. This method is somewhat similar to filtering by parameters in online stores. Although it does not require a huge dataset of information about users, it still requires a broad and detailed description of each product (Lops et al. 2011).

Since both approaches have their advantages and disadvantages, a combination of these algorithms—hybrid filtering—has appeared. This mixing allows to bypass the problems of both (Çano 2017).

Of particular interest is the use of recommender systems in software engineering. Such systems are used in all phases of development (Gašparič et al. 2015), as well as in various subsections of programming. For example, they can be used to assign status to pull requests (Azeem et al. 2020) and tags for questions (Zhang et al. 2018a), API selection (Cai et al. 2019; Thung et al. 2013; Xie et al. 2020), forum recommendation (Castro-Herrera et al. 2009), package suggestions (McMillan et al. 2012), bug detection (Ashok et al. 2009; Gomez et al. 2015), task selection (Wang et al. 2020), refactoring recommender (Lin et al. 2016), and many others. However, recommender systems have not yet been applied to define a set of metrics for a software project.

4.5 Metrics Recommender

Since data collectors, including Innometrics, collect data and present the user metrics in the form of graphs, it was necessary to create a recommender system to sift out unnecessary information on the application dashboard. The solution process for this task is as follows. The user enters the application, opens the tab with the GQM model, fills it—namely, enters the goals and questions for his project—and then clicks on the "Generate Metrics" button. The system processes all the text data it has previously received from other users. After that, it passes them to the recommender algorithm. It, in its turn, analyzes the data and displays the answer to the user by assigning the necessary metrics to the questions. For analysis, the system needs three things—a dataset, a way to process the data, and the recommender algorithm itself. The next sections examine these three components in more detail.

4.5.1   Dataset

Since the GQM-based metrics recommender is based on the analysis of textual data, firstly this data needs to be processed—brought to a common view to lower the sparsity level. Preprocessing is a data handling algorithm that solves exactly this problem. But there are many ways to process textual data. To choose the best one for our problem, we used a dataset that consists of many English sentences from Kagle: https://www.kaggle.com/theoviel/improve-your-score-with-some-text-preprocessing/notebook. With this dataset, we conducted several experiments, described in the next section.

Next, to evaluate the effectiveness of different recommender algorithms, we compiled our own second dataset, since no one had posted such a dataset in the public domain before us (Fitzgerald et al. 2011). To collect the dataset, we interviewed 35 developers of Innopolis. The developers, ranging from 21 to 32 years old with 1.5 to 6 years of work experience in different fields of software development, were included in the distribution.

4.5.2   Preprocessing

During the research, we found out that there are a limited number of steps used for text preprocessing, namely, (1) TF-IDF, (2) Stop words removal, (3) Tokenization, (4) Stemming, (5) Vectorization, (6) PoS and Lemmatization, and (7) Non-letter symbols removal. In order to determine the most suitable sequence for our problem, an experiment was conducted. Each possible sequence composed of these preprocessing steps was run 1000 times on the 500 sentences from the Kagle dataset. The machine used in the experiment had the following characteristics: Intel Core i5-8250U, 4GHz, 7862MiB RAM. The resulting mean runtime and standard deviation are shown in Table 4.1.

Multiple pairwise comparison tests using Tukey's method with a family error coefficient of 0.05 (Lee et al. 2018) show that the most efficient sequence is placed under letter B: (1) Non-letter symbols removal, (2) Tokenization, (3) Stop words removal, (4) PoS definition, (5) Lemmatization, and (6) TF-IDF. This is the sequence we have chosen for our system.

Table 4.1 Execution time for each combination

Group	Steps combination	Average time, ms	Std.dev., ms
A	Tokenization, Non-letters, Stop words, PoS and lemmatization	43.436	4.083
B	Non-letters, Tokenization, Stop words, PoS and lemmatization	41.003	1.068
C	Tokenization, PoS and lemmatization, Non-letters, Stop words	60.459	2.200
D	Tokenization, Non-letters, PoS and lemmatization, Stop words	59.080	2.667
E	Non-letters, Tokenization, PoS and lemmatization, Stop words	58.092	1.722
F	Tokenization, Stop words, Non-letters, PoS and lemmatization	45.810	0.757
G	Tokenization, Stop words, PoS and lemmatization, Non-letters	43.394	1.257
H	Tokenization, PoS and lemmatization, Stop words, Non-letters	57.518	0.848

4.5.3 Recommender Algorithm

The metrics recommender problem we identified earlier is a multi-label classification problem (Zhang et al. 2014), where multiple metrics can be assigned to each question. That is why we need to consider all types of multi-label classification algorithms in order to create a recommender algorithm. To quantify the effectiveness of each of them, we used the dataset collected from Innopolis employees, as mentioned in the "Dataset" subsection.

There exist several multi-label classification algorithms, which can be divided into two categories: *problem transformation* and *algorithm adaptation* (Tsoumakas et al. 2009). To choose from representatives of these two groups, we divided the dataset, described earlier, into 90% of train and 10% of the test set and evaluated all the multi-label algorithms from Table 4.2 on it. The results are shown in the same table.

The table shows that binary relevance is the best, so it was used for the implementation of the recommender algorithm.

Table 4.2 Multi-label algorithms comparison

	Problem transformation				Algorithm adaptation	
	Binary relevance	Classifier chains	Label powerset	RakelD	MLkNN	Decision trees
Accuracy	0.714	0.714	0.571	0.571	0.571	0.714
F1 score	0.888	0.888	0.476	0.384	0.384	0.526
Hamming loss	0.008	0.008	0.03	0.043	0.04	0.024

4.5.4   Conclusion

Based on our experiments, we developed a recommender algorithm for the "Inno-metrics" system. It was written in Java using the REST API technique. In one of the written endpoints, we put all the logic of the recommender system. Data received from users are first processed by the following sequence of preprocessing steps: (1) Non-letter symbols removal, (2) Tokenization, (3) Stop words removal, (4) PoS definition, (5) Lemmatization, and (6) TF-IDF. After that, they are passed to the recommender algorithm. It analyzes them and finally generates metrics suggestions for a new user. Thus, the user does not need to search for appropriate metrics from all of those available in the system. The algorithm automatically generates a goal-focused set of metrics that makes the best fit for each individual.

Chapter 5
Metrics Representation and Dashboards

Co-authored by Idel Ishbaev

Software development is unquestionably a difficult task. There are a variety of metrics that may be used to evaluate the development process and developers in order to improve this process. However, the usefulness of these indicators is determined by how they are visualized and presented. For these goals, information dashboards are handy. A dashboard is a "visual display of the most important information needed to achieve one or more objectives; consolidated and arranged on a single screen so the information can be monitored at a glance" (Few 2004).

Many studies have been conducted on dashboards, their purposes, visualization, and how to design one. They have been studied as Key Performance Indicators (KPI), scorecards (Kaplan et al. 1997), and Executive Information Systems (EIS) (Thierauf 1991) since the twentieth century, and they can all be treated in the same way (Few 2006). Furthermore, whereas dashboards were once studied in broad terms (Few 2004, 2006; Few et al. 2007; Pauwels et al. 2009), they are now explored in more specific areas, such as their usage in medicine (Boscardin et al. 2018), Continuous Software Engineering (Johanssen et al. 2017), and software development (López et al. 2021; Rahman et al. 2017).

Gaining a deeper understanding of these topics and analyzing them would help to improve development processes by providing valuable feedback (Hattie et al. 2007) and by creating better dashboards.

This chapter aims to better understand the dashboard's purposes and visualization approaches considering the dashboard's audience (developers and managers). In addition, it aims to create a faceted dashboard (Few et al. 2007), which means the same data can be represented in multiple ways for various people. This type of dashboard is also known as a tailored dashboard (Johanssen et al. 2019).

© The Author(s) 2023
A. Kruglov, G. Succi, *Developing Sustainable and Energy-Efficient Software Systems*, SpringerBriefs in Computer Science,
https://doi.org/10.1007/978-3-031-11658-2_5

5.1   Literature Review

A literature review is a crucial step in determining the study topic. It provides necessary background information, a clear picture of what has been developed and investigated, and its relevance and gaps in existing research. As a result, the following subjects were reviewed: dashboards in general, their types and goals, and visualization approaches.

5.1.1   Review of Literature on Dashboards

There are four levels of information, according to Savoie (2012): data, information, knowledge, and wisdom. Each level makes the previous one richer and more informative. The fist level is made up of facts with no meaning and is just input data. As stated by Few (2006), collecting, processing, and storing data is well explored, but there is "little progress in using that information effectively." As a result, to present data, it has to be turned into information, which is the second level of processing. To turn data into information, it must be organized and structured with a shared meaning. For example, we can organize the data into rows and columns, assigning titles and descriptions to them, and the data becomes meaningful as information. Furthermore, dashboards are the most effective approach to convey information (Savoie 2012).

EIS (Thierauf 1991), scorecards, and KPIs (Kaplan et al. 1997) have been studied since the 1990s. They are all used to support decision-making, measure performance, and monitor execution of activities, and according to Few (2006) dashboards appear to be synonymous or simply a new name for them. However, nowadays, the definition of dashboards by Few (2004) is the most used and common:

Visual display

of

the most Information needed to achieve one or more objectives

which

fits entirely on a single computer screen

so it can be

monitored at a glance.

It is evident from the definition that the dashboard's visual appearance, as well as its objectives, is very significant. It should deliver appropriate and reliable content in a straightforward and understandable manner to the end-user. According to Few (2006), most dashboards fail to communicate efficiently and effectively due to poorly designed implementation rather than a lack of technology.

Visualization of dashboards is essential not because of its beauty but because it can communicate with end-users with greater efficiency and richer meaning than plain text (Few 2006). As a result, visualization becomes more science than art because a successful dashboard is informed design, not just cute gauges, meters, and traffic lights (Few 2006).

Furthermore, while considering dashboard objectives, it is evident that different end-users would have varied objectives, requiring the development of different dashboards for each group of users. As a result, tailored dashboards are becoming increasingly useful (Few 2006; Johanssen et al. 2019), customized to meet individual needs to improve communication and suit the needs of users. In particular, faceted analytical displays give distinct views of the same data to different users for the purpose of analysis (Few et al. 2007); in other words, the same data is displayed in different ways.

5.1.2   Types of Dashboards

According to Eckerson (2010), there are three types of dashboards: operational, tactical, and strategic. Each type, from operational to tactical, has more complex data, which means that for the first type, simple data is used, and for the strategic type, more complex data for purposes of analysis.

Each type differs in its objectives, functionality, and end-users, which is the reason for different data abstraction levels. But even if they have different usages, they overlap in some sense, which means that the same dashboard can be used for various purposes and by other end-users. For example, front-line workers can use both tactical and operation types of dashboards and managers can use all three of them. Thus, each dashboard type has its own features, but there is no clear boundary between them (Table 5.1).

Operational level is mainly used by front-line workers to track operational processes, such as those involving people, tasks, events, and activities, as they occur.

Furthermore, there are two subtypes of the operational level: *detect-and-respond* and *incent-and-motivate*. The first subtype relates to monitoring activities or optimizing processes. The second subtype is a dashboard to increase workers' productivity by presenting the workers' or team's performance metrics.

Table 5.1 Dashboard types according to Eckerson (2010)

Type	Functionality	Users	Usage
Strategic dashboard	Monitor	Executives	Tracking progress (e.g., balanced scorecards)
Tactical dashboard	Analyze	Managers and analysts	Measuring and analyzing the performance. Most analytical dashboards
Operational dashboard	Detail	Front-line workers	Monitoring tracking processes

Most operational level dashboards display metrics of low-level processes; they contain detailed data or sometimes are slightly summarized. Furthermore, the dashboards often offer only one level of data with no drill-down functionality and provide the most up-to-date information. The dashboards look like automobile dashboards with alerts, dials, and gauges.

Tactical level is used to optimize business processes and to analyze performance against goals. Dashboards emphasize analysis, and monitoring is also available. In most cases, the dashboard looks like an analytical or functional dashboard containing tables and charts describing what happened in the past. Also, it is worth mentioning that usually for tactical-level dashboards different users have different data presented depending on their role.

Interaction with charts and tables is a regular feature at the operational level. Drill-down, filters, sorting, changing views, pop-ups (Few 2006), and other features make it easier to interact with the dashboard and improve the user experience.

The dashboards used by mid-level managers and their appearance are somewhere between operational and strategic levels, allowing users to keep track of different processes and data in one spot.

Strategic level is mostly used by executives to review the progress toward strategic goals once a month or more rarely. In summary, the first two levels measure processes to understand what is happening now or in the short term, but the strategic level deals with long-term strategies.

Furthermore, some research includes a fourth type: **analytical**. It contains a large amount of complex data and what-if scenarios to assist executives in their analysis and planning (Nadj et al. 2020).

In addition, dashboards can also be classified as static (read-only) and interactive. Despite that, Few (2006) states that providing different varieties of data is meaningless, and nowadays static dashboards are not relevant anymore. Interactive dashboards can help to handle chunks of information effectively considering the growth of complexity and amount of data (Nadj et al. 2020).

5.1.3   Purposes/Objectives of Dashboards

There are four main purposes of dashboards according to Pauwels et al. (2009): consistency, monitoring, planning, and communication.

- **Consistency**—indicates an organization's procedures, measures, and measurements.
- **Monitoring**—monitor and evaluate performance. Such dashboards are early performance indicators of performance and let companies detect and react.
- **Planning**—strategic planning.
- **Communication**—share information about performance, organization values as performance, etc.

However, Rahman et al. (2017) propose a fifth purpose of dashboards—**analysis**, which is used to analyze personal and companies' performance and is similar to the monitoring purpose of Pauwels et al. (2009) but more precise.

5.1.4   Visualization Methods of Dashboards

In the study by Yigitbasioglu et al. (2012), the authors underline the importance of interaction with a dashboard. Their research on dashboard graphical user interfaces distinguished two categories of design features: visual and functional.

Visual features refer to how data is displayed to the user; they influence how effectively and efficiently data is presented, and they directly affect the time for perceiving information. Inappropriate use of visual effects, such as varying surface styles, expanding the number and ranges of objects, overwhelming 3D objects, and non-value-adding frames, can make the understanding process more difficult. Gridlines inside charts, a high data-ink ratio, and the elimination of non-data-ink components in charts are all examples of improvements.
"Data-ink ratio is a parameter that defines the relationship of ink used to illustrate data to the overall ink leveraged to represent the chart" (Nadj et al. 2020).

An example of poor visual features is inappropriate use of color or data-ink ratio, which will distract or confuse users, for example, using yellow and red too often may attract attention and also may lead to the impossibility of highlighting errors or critical information (Nadj et al. 2020).
Green, yellow, and red should represent acceptable, satisfactory, and poor performance/alarms, respectively (Few 2006).

Functional features describe what the dashboard can do. Such features include pointing and clicking interactivity, which enables rolling down and up, filtering, sorting, brushing, illustrating more data, and additional information on pointing.

Such features are a step toward interactive dashboards, in which the user is actively participating in the data analysis process. However, the user's effort to interact can lengthen the analysis process or have a negative impact on decision-making (Nadj et al. 2020).

An example of a poor functional feature is dashboards which fail to provide needed functionality to a user who cannot gain enough information (e.g., to analyze or plan) from dashboards due to a lack of these features.

Few (2006) also includes standard practices in his study, such as visual and functional features:

Common features:

- Using charts, tables, speedometer widgets for graphical representation
- Dividing the full set of data to individual views
- "Digital cockpit"—summary of performance by color-coded light indicator
- Using gauges with traffic-light colors

In addition, in the study by López et al. (2021), the authors provide different views and different kinds of charts to analyze the performance and distinguish different levels of abstraction to visualize the same data. According to the study, high-level strategic indicators are effective and improve decision-making processes.

- Process performance strategic indicators (SI)—gauge chart showing the SI assessment value
- Detailed SI—radar chart, quality factors (QF) for the SI assessment
- Factors—radar chart, metrics for the QF assessment
- Historical data view for metrics—line chart, metrics assessments

5.2 Methodology and Implementation

In this chapter, knowledge gathered from various studies is assessed and applied to the Innometrics project considering its objectives and constraints. In order to develop a visualization of the dashboard, the following steps were proposed.

- Define audience, end-users
- Define objectives, constraints
- Define purposes, Fig. 5.1
- Define type, Fig. 5.1
- Determine visual and functional features (Yigitbasioglu et al. 2012) for visualization, Table 5.2
- Develop architecture

5.2.1 Innometrics Project

Innometrics is a project that tracks, evaluates, and analyzes the software development process. This system provides a visualization of users' working activity statistics.

Fig. 5.1 Purposes (Pauwels
et al. 2009; Rahman et al.
2017) and types (Eckerson
2010; Few 2006; Johanssen
et al. 2017, 2019; Nadj et al.
2020) of dashboards

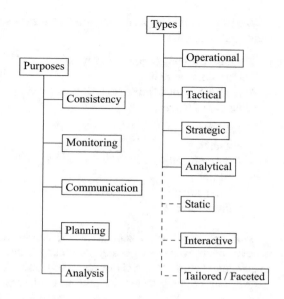

Table 5.2 Visual and functional features (Eckerson 2010; Few 2004, 2006; Nadj et al. 2020; Rahman et al. 2017)

Visual	• Fit in single screen • Gridline overlay within charts • Color-coded light indicator • Traffic-light colors • High data-ink ratio • Grid overlay • Full set of data to individual views

Functional	• Drill down/up
	• Sorting
	• Brushing/Filtering
	• Zoom
	• Tooltips/Pop-ups
	• Range settings
	• Customization
	• Presentation format type
	
	  – Tabular Information (for extracting specific values)
	  – Graphical representation:
	    · Different types of charts
	    · Charts with historical data
	    · Charts showing the SI assessment value

The project collects, analyzes, and visualizes users' activity data and developers' code quality metrics:

- Top applications per person daily
- Accumulated activities
- Accumulated total time spent
- Category of activities
    - Development
    - Education
    - Communication
    - Utilities
    - Management
    - Entertainment

This project aims to keep track of, assess, and evaluate developers and the development process in general. A robust dashboard, which is "such a powerful management tool" (Pauwels et al. 2009), must be designed to visualize data as metrics and communicate with end-users effectively and efficiently. It effectively communicates with the target user by presenting data as information. As noted in the review, we present data in dashboards since it is the most efficient and effective approach to convey data as information and communicate with users. However, to design such a dashboard, we examined its goals and who the target audience is.

There are two types of end-users in the project, each with a different purpose, managerial level, and request for different types of information from dashboards. The project's primary audience are developers and managers (Fig. 5.2).

As a result, the challenge was to deliver information to both types of users in an effective and efficient manner. We created two unique dashboard visualizations for these purposes, each with a different level of data abstraction (López et al. 2021) and visualization elements (Yigitbasioglu et al. 2012). To put it another way, it will be a **faceted** dashboard. It offers a distinct view for developers that will satisfy front-line workers' requirements. For managers, it has another visualization with different objectives, and it *delivers another piece of information using the same data*. Moreover, considering that the project is growing and will have more metrics and graphics in the future, extensible architecture was developed.

Fig. 5.2 Types of end-users

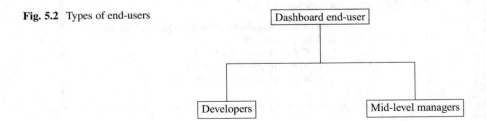

To decide how to visualize data properly, we first examined the objectives of both types of users, and then selected a type of dashboard and appropriate visual and functional features.

5.2.2 Visualization for Developers

Developers are the first group of users. They are front-line employees that require the most up-to-date performance metrics for monitoring rather than historical metrics for analysis. As a result, the dashboard's purposes are *analysis* and *monitor*, and its types are *operational*, with subtype *incent-and-motivate*. Considering that, there are less historical data and more Process Performance strategic indicators (gauges) (López et al. 2021) in the dashboard. Furthermore, it is more static than interactive because unnecessary interactive features can distract users (Nadj et al. 2020); yet, it does provide some interactivity choices to improve user experience.

The purpose, type, and features for developers' dashboard may be found in the Creftab (Table 5.3).

5.2.3 Visualization for Managers

The second group of users is mid-level managers—decision-makers who monitor and analyze employees' performance and development processes. Thus, the dashboard has *monitor* and *communication* purposes and tactical type. It is also fully interactive, making it more analytical and assisting users in better comprehending complex data. In Table 5.4 type, purposes, and features for managers' dashboards can be observed.

Table 5.3 Dashboard for developers

Purpose	• Analysis (Rahman et al., 2017) • Monitor (Pauwels et al., 2009)
Type	• Operational—detect-and-respond (Eckerson, 2010) • Partly interactive
Functional features	• Gauges • Chart showing the SI assessment value • Speedometer look like widgets with color indicators
Visual	• Color-coded light indicator

Table 5.4 Dashboard for managers

Purpose	• Monitor (Pauwels et al., 2009) • Communication (Pauwels et al., 2009)
Type	• Tactical (Eckerson, 2010) • Interactive
Functional features	• Tabular Information • Historical data • Range settings • Interaction functionality (filtering, hiding, sorting, drill down/up)

Table 5.5 Common features for developers' and managers' dashboards

Visual	• Fit in single screen • Gridline overlay within charts • Traffic-light colors • High data-ink ratio • Grid overlay • Full set of data to individual views
Functional	• Drill down/up • Sorting • Brushing/Filtering • Zoom • Tooltips/Pop-ups • Customization • Presentation format type (some types of charts)

5.2.4   Common Visual and Functional Features

Since *operational* and *tactical* types that we determined for both dashboards sometimes overlap, some features are shared (Eckerson 2010), especially visual features, which affect how effectively and efficiently data is presented. In Table 5.5 these features can be observed.

5.2.5   Architecture, Implementation

Another problem was to develop a dashboard that was extensible and maintainable as the project progressed and more metrics and graphics were added. The goal was to provide front-end extensibility that allowed developers to delete, add, and change widgets, graphics, and other visualized data easily, without relying on other layers. Several design patterns and principles can be used to create a dashboard on the front-end layer that is easily expandable and maintainable. The Mediator Design Pattern can be utilized in object-oriented programming (OOP) (Gamma et al. 1995).

The ReactJS framework was used to build the user interface. Thus, we rely on Functional Programming (FP) since the framework relies on Functional components for modern React applications (Banks et al. 2017), and it was not possible to use the Mediator Design Pattern in its pure form.

Functional components were used, which means that components were defined as functions (not as classes). Functions have different design patterns and principles than OOP. We defined low-level functions and then applied composition (Banks et al. 2017). With the help of this, simple standalone functions are consolidated into one big dashboard system.

Moreover, we took the idea from the mediator pattern and created a mediator component that comprised low-level function components (Wieruch 2022). The mediator component took care of preprocessing data (turning data into metrics) and setting configuration data for low-level functions. After configuration components create cards with the following fields for each widget:

- id
- name
- type (*used to distribute to exact widget, for example, **line graph***)
- API (*function to fetch data*)
- *some other configuration information

The mediator component distributes data to low-level components based on the **type** field. As a result, low-level graphical representation components deal only with ready input data and can be reused (see Fig. 5.3). Thus, only configuration components can be updated to maintain the dashboard.

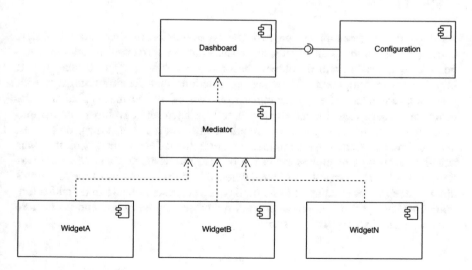

Fig. 5.3 Components of dashboard

In Fig. 5.3 the structure of the dashboard can be observed:

- Dashboard—the highest abstraction level, which comprises lower-level components. It deals with the creation of configuration cards, which are then passed on to the mediator.
- Configuration—a component that generates cards for each widget, each with fields such as name, type, and API data.
- Mediator—component that receives configuration cards and distributes them to the widgets based on their types.
- WidgetA … WidgetN—the lowest-level components that receive preprocessed data and present it in a certain way based on the user's role.

As a result, updating existing widgets or adding new graphics can be accomplished in a few simple steps, which aligns with our goal of creating a dashboard that is easy to extend and manage.

Steps to edit or add new widgets:

1. Edit configuration component (edit or add new card):
   - Specify the type that the mediator will use to pass to the exact widget.
   - Update id, name, etc.
   - Set the default location for it to appear.

2. *If necessary, create a preprocessing function (to transform data into a form that can be used by a widget component).
3. *Create new widget (new representation) if needed.

5.2.6   Conclusion

As the software development process and its evaluation become more complex, understanding the purposes, types, and visualization approaches of tailored dashboards for managers and developers becomes an essential topic. Hence, it will improve the development of metrics presentations that provide end-users with more relevant data. After reviewing various works, it became evident that the dashboard requires specific representation for managers and developers, taking into account their respective goals and requirements. As a result, types, objectives, and aesthetic aspects were examined in order to design a dashboard that was suited to each type of end-user. On top of that, the dashboard's architecture was designed to be easily maintainable and extensible since it was one of the research's aims. A deep understanding of dashboard types, purposes, visuals, and architecture allows assessing the development process and presenting metrics to end-users more accurately and in a practical manner.

Chapter 6
Architecture of AISEMA System

Co-authored by Xavier Vasquez

At an industrial level, data collection is an important task, since, from these, it is possible to gather information on the current state of the processes, identify possible problems, or find mechanisms to be able to optimize stages of the production process, and the case of software production processes is not exempt from this type of analysis.

Over time, the data collection process has evolved, going from an initial stage of manual and systematic collection carried out by a person, which could reach the point of even hindering or slowing down the process under study, to today where we can incorporate automated data collection mechanisms, where human intervention is minimal and therefore generates a minimal impact on the development of the process. In our particular case, it is a study of the software development process.

Based on the situation raised above, in this section we will describe from a high-level perspective the main components that must be included in the design of an Automated In-process Software Engineering Measurement and Analysis (AISEMA) system, which broadly consists of one or more components responsible for collecting data in a noninvasive way, a component in charge of centralizing the collected data, and a third component in charge of presenting indicators or other types of information generated from the previously collected data.

© The Author(s) 2023
A. Kruglov, G. Succi, *Developing Sustainable and Energy-Efficient Software Systems*, SpringerBriefs in Computer Science,
https://doi.org/10.1007/978-3-031-11658-2_6

6.1   Data Collectors

6.1.1   *Quality Attributes*

We will start by describing one of the key components of an AISEMA system, the data collection component, which must meet the following quality attributes:

- *Extensibility* is necessary since, over time, the incorporation of new metrics could become a need; due to that, it is important that our design allows the inclusion of new modules in a simple way.
- *Performance* is one of the fundamental pillars in design, since we want our data collector to have the least possible impact in the execution of daily activities.
- *Reliability* is another point to highlight, since, in order to carry out an adequate analysis, it is necessary for our component to be able to obtain the data correctly and precisely all the time, and these data must be stored and transmitted as expected.
- *Security* is a point that many could overlook; however, depending on the degree of sensitivity of the data captured, security plays an important role in our design, since many times we will be able to capture information about individuals or work groups, which we would not want to see compromised, since we do not know what kind of manipulation could be carried out on them.

6.1.2   *Features*

Once the quality attributes of the data collection components have been defined, let us see in detail the desired features; for this particular case, we will analyze the data collectors developed for the project called Innometrics, which from a high-level perspective is responsible for collecting data on resource utilization during the software development process.

As mentioned above, the main feature of the data collector is to monitor the impact that each application running on the developer's computer has on the use of available resources. For example, we want to be able to monitor CPU usage, GPU usage, RAM, and I/O operations, as this will help us in the future in making our predictions on energy consumption or to predict the number of computational resources needed to run a certain project.

On the other hand, it is also required to monitor the application that runs in the foreground, so that it is possible to try to understand which activity the user performs and in turn the time that the user spends actively on it (Fig. 6.1). Also, for reasons of transparency, it is necessary to provide access to the user for the data that has been collected, either historically or in real time, so a minimal graphical interface will be required to display this type of information. In addition, since the data collection is intended to be noninvasive and we would not like to disturb the normal execution of

Fig. 6.1 Innometrics monitor

the developers' activities, it will be necessary to include a control panel with which the data collection period can be adjusted, and the periodicity with which the data is synchronized with the central database (Fig. 6.2).

6.1.3   Internal Design

Up to this point, we have already defined the bases of our system to take the next step, to describe the architectural design that our system should have. We are going to detail it starting from the highest level components until we reach the detail of each of them. Also it should be clarified that the design presented can be taken as a guide with good practices and which can be improved in various ways.

We can divide our data collection application into four different components:

- Graphic interface
- Data collectors

Fig. 6.2 Innometrics monitor

- Persistence layer
- API controller

6.1.3.1 Graphic Interface

This component is mainly responsible for presenting the collected data, giving access to the configuration section and a summary view of the data that is monitored in real time.

However, it is this same component which is responsible for managing the different execution threads, which are used to track each of the different metrics that we want to monitor, so in this way, we can isolate each one of the follow-up processes, without their execution being limited or influenced by any of the other threads.

And it is in this same way that an additional thread is also included, which is responsible for synchronizing the data to the central database and in turn monitoring in case any notification is received from the backend, either to notify the user or as a request to update the component.

6.1.3.2 Data Collectors

In order to provide extensibility to the system, the data collection processes have been separated into an independent module, which provides the necessary interfaces so that more metrics can be incorporated later. In Listing 6.1, we can see a code snippet that shows the implementation for Windows operating systems of the function which generates the report on all the processes that are being executed in the system.

This component (Fig. 6.3) is able to:

- Monitor equipment battery status information
- Track the window on which the user actively performs his task
- Collect metrics on each process in terms of resource utilization, as:
  - GPU
  - CPU
  - RAM
  - Network usage
  - I/O operations

6.1.3.3 Persistence Layer and API Controller

Finally, we have two complementary modules, which are the persistence layer and the API controller. In the case of the persistence layer, it implements the necessary operations for the storage and management of the data collected locally on the user's device. On the other hand, the API controller is responsible for defining and implementing the interfaces that are used for communication with the backend. And it is in this way that we can decouple our data collector from any database that we need to use and also from the API that is used to store the information.

6.2 Backend System

We have already described the main characteristics that the data collection agents must have and introduced a high-level design for them, and it is necessary to do the same with the complementary part within the AISEMA scheme.

In this case, we are talking about a component which will help us to consolidate the data that has already been collected by those agents, which we will call backend.

Listing 6.1 Data collector snippet

```
public CollectorProcessReport GetCurrentProcessReport(
    DateTime measurementTime)
{
    log.Info("Generation process report...");
    var myReport = new CollectorProcessReport();

var currentWindows = OpenWindowGetter.
    GetOpenedWindowsProcessesInfo();
PowerStatus pwr = SystemInformation.PowerStatus;
BatteryInformation batteryInfo = BatteryInfo.
    GetBatteryInformation();

// get IP address of host computer
var myIp = GetIpAddress();

// get mac address of host machine
var firstMacAddress = GetMACAddress();

foreach (var w in currentWindows)
{
    var wi = w.Value;
    var pi = w.Value.ProcessInfo;

    var myProcess = new CollectorProcess
    {
        ProcessName = pi.ProcessName,
        ProcessType = "OS",
        WindowsTitle = wi.WindowTitle,
        BrowserUrl = "",
        IpAddress = myIp,
        MacAddress = firstMacAddress,
        UserName = "",
        Description = pi.MainModuleDescription,
        Status = "0",
        mainAppPath = pi.MainModulePath,
        PID = pi.ProcessId.ToString(),
        collectedTime = measurementTime
    };

    float estimatedChargeRemaining = (float)
        batteryInfo.CurrentCapacity /
    (float)batteryInfo.FullChargeCapacity;
```

```
estimatedChargeRemaining =
    estimatedChargeRemaining > 100.0 ?
100 :  estimatedChargeRemaining;

...

myProcess.Measurements.Add(new ProcessMetrics
{
    MeasurementType = "2", // "BatteryStatus",
    Value = pwr.BatteryChargeStatus.ToString(),
    CapturedTime = measurementTime
});
...

myProcess.Measurements.Add(new ProcessMetrics
{
    MeasurementType = "13", // "
        designMaxCapacityBattery",
    Value = batteryInfo.DesignedMaxCapacity.
        ToString(CultureInfo.InvariantCulture),
    CapturedTime = measurementTime
});

myReport.processes.Add(myProcess);
}

return myReport;
}
```

6.2.1 Quality Attributes

It is because of the above that we must have an ecosystem of services that support these operations, which must meet at least the following quality attributes:

- *Compatibility*: This section is very important, since on some occasions we could find ourselves with different technologies, so it is important to use a communication protocol that is widely used in most platforms, in addition to being able to have controls over the version of the API and the data collectors that are deployed, so we can know if any of the components are out of date and request the end-user to perform an update or perform the update unattended.
- *Reliability*, in addition to our system being able to support connectivity with various platforms, it is also important to guarantee that the backend will continue to function even in less favorable conditions, such as a high transactional load, tolerating possible failures either in communication or regarding the transmitted data.

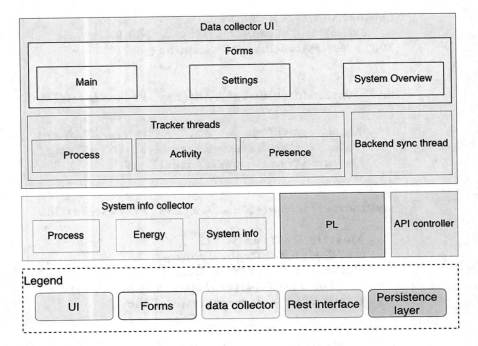

Fig. 6.3 Data collector internal design

- *Security*: Given the sensitivity of the stored data, it is important to implement an adequate security protocol that helps us to prevent possible malicious use of the information.
- *Maintainability*: In terms of maintainability, it is important that there is good modularity in the system, since this helps us to expand the frontiers of the initial implementation, to be able to add new functionalities, or to achieve integrations with other systems in the future.

In this case, the performance of the system could go into the background, since, due to what is implemented in the data collector, we have a local backup of the data, so in case the system is not capable of processing all transactions, these could be attended to later.

6.2.2   Features

We can detail the desired characteristics as follows:

- It is necessary to have an API that serves us mainly to be able to receive the information that has been collected through the data collectors.

- A system for the authentication and authorization of system users, since it is necessary to have different levels of authorization; in our case, it is necessary to have developers, managers, and system administrators.
- A series of dedicated APIs for displaying information on the system's dashboard.
- In addition to this, it is necessary to have a component that allows us to have integration with external systems in order to collect data from the software development process that cannot be collected directly on the development team's devices.

6.2.3   Internal Design

6.2.3.1   Main Server

In the main server, as we can see in Fig. 6.4, we have a set of services that support us in order to provide the essential functionalities for data collectors and dashboards, as detailed below:

- *DataCollectorAPI*: This service is in charge of providing the methods that are consumed by the data collectors, in which reports with the collected data are periodically sent, and it also provides external authentication services, which will be used by the dashboard and by the data collectors themselves. It also provides the interfaces to be able to adjust the system configurations and user management, and these tasks will be executed from the dashboard by those administrator users.
- *Authorization service*: On the other hand, for reasons of reuse and scaling, we have decided to implement user authentication and authorization in an independent service, so that if necessary we can have multiple instances of this service and any service of ours. The ecosystem can make use of the services provided.
- *Activity collector service*: However, the service that will bear the greatest transactional load will be the activity collection service. This service will basically be in charge of processing the reports sent by the data collectors and generating the data sets that are necessary for generating the graphs shown in the dashboard; in the same way, by having this service independently, we can have the facility to scale the system more easily if this is required.

Also note that these services are deployed in Docker containers, which help us scale in a very simple way, and in turn have a service registration server. In this case, we're talking about the Eureka server, which provides tools for automatic service discovery and has a load balancing mechanism.

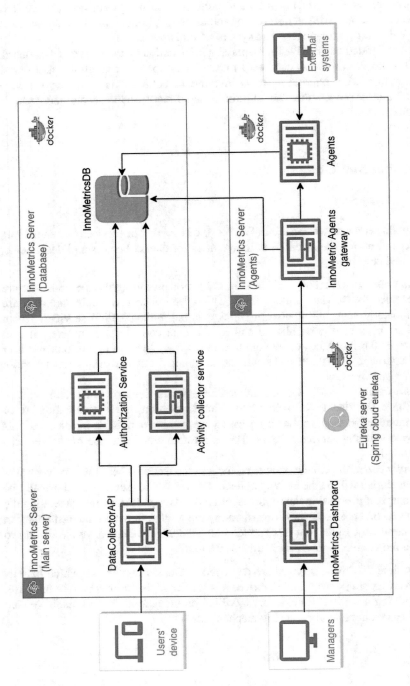

Fig. 6.4 Backend internal design

6.2.3.2   Database

Regarding the database, we can mention that we have a PostgreSQL implementation, which is divided into two different sections: 1) a database with transactional data and data about users, and projects, and 2) additional configurations of both the system and integrations with external systems.

6.2.3.3   External Agents

In terms of external agents, there is an additional server, which has the services for direct integration with external systems, for example, consuming REST services and collecting the necessary information related to a specific project.

Also as an additional mechanism, it is capable of being able to connect directly to the databases of external agents, since in some cases the integration can be done directly via API or, in other cases, it is necessary to install plugins that will have their own database.

6.3   Conclusion

As we have seen throughout the chapter, we have been able to describe two big important components in the architecture of the AISEMA system, where it is very important to have a good design for the data collectors because they can hinder the activities of the development team if the appropriate measures are not taken. It is also worth noting that it is necessary to calibrate both the process scanning and data sending periods to the backend in order to achieve accurate data sampling without overloading the system. For our particular case, through numerous experiments, we were able to determine that collecting data every 2 minutes and synchronizing with the central database every 10 minutes provides us with an acceptable level of accuracy.

Regarding the backend, we note that one of the main advantages of the system is its flexibility in terms of the many types of integration that can be supported and the ease of scaling at peak transactions, for which it is important to pre-measure the number of simultaneous users that will be working in the system.

References

Alsultanny, Yas A. 2018. Green IT readiness and directions of power consumption. In *Green computing strategies for competitive advantage and business sustainability*, 40–61. IGI Global.

Amsel, Nadine et al. (2010). Green tracker. In ACM.

Armenise, Valentina. 2015. Continuous delivery with Jenkins: Jenkins solutions to implement continuous delivery. In *2015 IEEE/ACM 3rd International Workshop on Release Engineering*, 24–27. Piscataway: IEEE.

Ashok, B. et al. 2009. DebugAdvisor: A recommender system for debugging. In *Proceedings of the 7th Joint Meeting of the European Software Engineering Conference and the ACM SIGSOFT Symposium on The Foundations of Software Engineering*. ESEC/FSE '09, 373–382. Amsterdam: Association for Computing Machinery.

Aversano, Lerina et al. 2017. Analysis of the documentation of ERP software projects. *Procedia Computer Science* 121: 423–430.

Azeem, Muhammad Ilyas et al. 2020. Action-based recommendation in pull-request development. In *Proceedings of the International Conference on Software and System Processes*. ICSSP '20, 115–124. Seoul: Association for Computing Machinery.

Bajaj, Anu et al. 2019. A systematic literature review of test case prioritization using genetic algorithms. *IEEE Access* 7: 126355–126375.

Banks, Alex et al. 2017. *Learning React: functional web development with React and Redux*. Sebastopol: O'Reilly Media.

Basili, Victor R et al. 1996. A validation of object-oriented design metrics as quality indicators. *IEEE Transactions on Software Engineering* 22(10): 751–761.

Basili, Victor R. et al. 1994. *The goal question metric approach*, vol. I. New York: Wiley.

Bekaroo, Girish et al. 2016. Power consumption of the Raspberry Pi: A comparative analysis. In *2016 IEEE International Conference on Emerging Technologies and Innovative Business Practices for the Transformation of Societies (EmergiTech)*, 361–366. Piscataway: IEEE.

Bharathi, R. et al. 2015. A framework for the estimation of OO software reliability using design complexity metrics. In *2015 International Conference on Trends in Automation, Communications and Computing Technology (I-TACT-15)*, 1–7. Piscataway: IEEE.

Boscardin, Christy et al. 2018. Twelve tips to promote successful development of a learner performance dashboard within a medical education program. *Medical Teacher* 40(8): 855–861.

Brown, Len et al. 2006. Linux* laptop battery life. In *Proc. of the Linux Symposium*, 127–146. Citeseer.

Cai, Liang et al. 2019. BIKER: A tool for bi-information source based API method recommendation. In *Proceedings of the 2019 27th ACM Joint Meeting on European Software Engineering*

© The Author(s) 2023

A. Kruglov, G. Succi, *Developing Sustainable and Energy-Efficient Software Systems*, SpringerBriefs in Computer Science, https://doi.org/10.1007/978-3-031-11658-2

Conference and Symposium on the Foundations of Software Engineering. ESEC/FSE 2019, 1075–1079. Tallinn: Association for Computing Machinery.

Çano, Erion. 2017. Hybrid recommender systems: A systematic literature review. *Intelligent Data Analysis* 21: 1487–1524.

Castro-Herrera, Carlos et al. 2009. A recommender system for requirements elicitation in large-scale software projects. In *Proceedings of the 2009 ACM Symposium on Applied Computing*. SAC '09, 1419–1426. Honolulu: Association for Computing Machinery.

Chandola, Varun et al. 2009. Anomaly detection: A survey. *ACM Computing Surveys* 41(3): 15.

Chen, Xuhui et al. 2017. Real-time personalized cardiac arrhythmia detection and diagnosis: A cloud computing architecture. In *2017 IEEE EMBS International Conference on Biomedical & Health Informatics (BHI)*, 201–204. Piscataway: IEEE.

Ciancarini, Paolo et al. 2020. Analysis of energy consumption of software development process entities. *Electronics* 9: 1678.

Conti, Mauro et al. 2016a. Mind the plug! Laptop-user recognition through power consumption. In *Proceedings of the 2nd ACM International Workshop on IoT Privacy, Trust, and Security*. IoTPTS '16, 37–44. Xi'an: Association for Computing Machinery.

Conti, Mauro et al. 2016b. Mind the plug! Laptop-user recognition through power consumption. In *Proceedings of the 2nd ACM International Workshop on IoT Privacy, Trust, and Security*, 37–44.

Davis, Alan M. 1988. A taxonomy for the early stages of the software development life cycle. *Journal of Systems and Software* 8(4): 297–311.

Di Nucci, Dario et al. 2017. Software-based energy profiling of android apps: Simple, efficient and reliable? In *2017 IEEE 24th International Conference on Software Analysis, Evolution and Reengineering (SANER)*, 103–114. Piscataway: IEEE.

Do, Thanh et al. 2009. ptop: A process-level power profiling tool. In *in Proceedings of the 2nd Workshop on Power Aware Computing and Systems (HotPower'09)*.

Dorogush, Anna Veronika et al. 2018. CatBoost: gradient boosting with categorical features support. arXiv preprint arXiv:1810.11363.

Eckerson, Wayne W. 2010. *Performance dashboards: measuring, monitoring, and managing your business*, 101–122. New York: Wiley.

Ergasheva, Shokhista et al. 2020. Metrics of energy consumption in software systems: A systematic literature review. In *IOP Conference Series: Earth and Environmental Science*. Vol. 431, 012051. Bristol: IOP Publishing.

Fenton, Norman et al. 1997. *Software metrics: A rigorous and practical approach*, 2nd ed. London: International Thomson Computer Press.

Few, Stephen, 2004. Dashboard confusion. perceptual edge. In *Verfügbar unter*. https://slidelegend. com/dashboard-confusion-perceptual-edge_59c2ed291723dd5142fc7e6e.html. Accessed 20 January 2021.

Few, Stephen. 2006. *Information dashboard design: The effective visual communication of data*. Vol. 2. Sebastopol: O'Reilly.

Few, Stephen et al. 2007. Dashboard confusion revisited. In *Perceptual Edge*, 1–6.

Fitzgerald, Brian et al. 2011. *Adopting open source software: A practical guide*. Cambridge, MA: The MIT Press.

Gamma, Erich et al. 1995. *Design patterns: Elements of reusable object-oriented software*. Pearson Deutschland GmbH.

Gašparič, Marko et al. 2015. What recommendation systems for software engineering recommend: a systematic literature review. *Journal of Systems and Software* 113: 101–113.

Gomez, Maria et al. 2015. A recommender system of buggy app checkers for app store moderators. In *Proceedings of the Second ACM International Conference on Mobile Software Engineering and Systems*. MOBILESoft '15, 1–11. Florence: IEEE Press.

Goraczko, Michel. 2010. *Joulemeter: Computational Energy Measurement and Optimization*. https://www.microsoft.com/en-us/research/project/joulemeter-computational-energy-measurement-and-optimization/. Accessed 8 October 2021.

Guaman, Daniel et al. 2017. SonarQube as a tool to identify software metrics and technical debt in the source code through static analysis. In *Proceedings of 2017 the 7th International Workshop on Computer Science and Engineering*. WCSE.

Hattie, John et al. 2007. The power of feedback. *Review of Educational Research* 77(1): 81–112. Eprint: https://doi.org/10.3102/003465430298487.

Hota, Chinmay et al. 2019. An empirical analysis on effectiveness of source code metrics for aging related bug prediction. In *Proceedings of the 25th International Conference on Distributed Multimedia Systems*. KSI Research Inc. and Knowledge Systems Institute Graduate School.

Humphrey, Watts. 2005. *PSP: A self-improvement process for software engineers*. Reading, MA: Addison-Wesley Professional.

Isinkaye, F.O. et al. 2015. Recommendation systems: Principles, methods and evaluation. *Egyptian Informatics Journal* 16(3): 261–273.

Janes, Andrea et al. 2014. *Lean software development in action*. Berlin: Springer.

Johanssen, Jan Ole et al. 2017. Towards the visualization of usage and decision knowledge in continuous software engineering. In *2017 IEEE Working Conference on Software Visualization (VISSOFT)*. Piscataway: IEEE.

Johanssen, Jan Ole et al. 2019. Tailored information dashboards: A systematic mapping of the literature. In *Proceedings of the XX International Conference on Human Computer Interaction*, 1–8.

Johnson, P.M. et al. 2003. Beyond the personal software process: Metrics collection and analysis for the differently disciplined. In *25th International Conference on Software Engineering, 2003. Proceedings*. Piscataway: IEEE.

Joulemeter. 2010. *Joule meter*. https://www.microsoft.com/en-us/research/project/joulemeter-computational-energy-measurement-and-optimization/. Accessed 10 April 2022.

Kabir, M Firoz et al. 2018. Cyber security challenges: An efficient intrusion detection system design. In *2018 international young engineers forum (YEF-ECE)*, 19–24. Piscataway: IEEE.

Kaplan, Robert S. et al. 1997. *Balanced scorecard*. Schäffer-Poeschel.

Kumar, Lov et al. 2016. Empirical validation for effectiveness of fault prediction technique based on cost analysis framework. *International Journal of System Assurance Engineering and Management* 8(S2): 1055–1068.

Kumar, Prathipati Ratna et al. 2017. A novel probabilistic-ABC based boosting model for software defect detection. In *2017 International Conference on Innovations in Information, Embedded and Communication Systems (ICIIECS)*, 1–6. Piscataway: IEEE.

Lee, Sangseok et al. 2018. What is the proper way to apply the multiple comparison test? *Korean Journal of Anesthesiology* 71(5): 353–360.

Li, Sheng et al. 2009. McPAT. New York: ACM Press.

Li, Tao et al. 2003. Run-time modeling and estimation of operating system power consumption. In *Proceedings of the 2003 ACM SIGMETRICS International Conference on Measurement and Modeling of Computer Systems*, 160–171.

Lin, Yun et al. 2016. Interactive and guided architectural refactoring with search-based recommendation. In *Proceedings of the 2016 24th ACM SIG-SOFT International Symposium on Foundations of Software Engineering*. FSE 2016, 535–546. Seattle: Association for Computing Machinery.

Liu, Weifeng et al. 2020. Improving the energy efficiency of data-intensive applications running on clusters. *International Journal of Parallel, Emergent and Distributed Systems* 35(3): 246–259.

López, L. et al. 2021. QaSD: A quality-aware strategic dashboard for supporting decision makers in agile software development. *Science of Computer Programming* 202: 102568.

Lops, Pasquale et al. 2011. Content-based recommender systems: State of the art and trends. In *Recommender Systems Handbook*, 73–105.

Machado, Bruno N. et al. 2016. SBSTFrame: A framework to search-based software testing. In *2016 IEEE International Conference on Systems, Man, and Cybernetics (SMC)*. Piscataway: IEEE.

Mahesri, Aqeel et al. 2004. Power consumption breakdown on a modern laptop. In *International Workshop on Power-Aware Computer Systems*, 165–180. Berlin: Springer.

Martı, Luis et al. 2015. Anomaly detection based on sensor data in petroleum industry applications. *Sensors* 15(2): 2774–2797.

Mazouz, Abdelhafid et al. 2017. An incremental methodology for energy measurement and modeling. In *Proceedings of the 8th ACM/SPEC on International Conference on Performance Engineering*, 15–26.

McKay, Timothy et al. 2019. *Intel power gadget*. https://software.intel.com/en-us/articles/intel-power-gadget-20. Accessed 9 October 2021.

McMillan, Collin et al. 2012. Recommending source code for use in rapid software prototypes. In *Proceedings of the 34th International Conference on Software Engineering*. ICSE '12, 848–858. Zurich: IEEE Press.

Nadj, Mario et al. 2020. The effect of interactive analytical dashboard features on situation awareness and task performance. *Decision Support Systems* 135: 113322.

Palomba, Fabio et al. 2019. On the impact of code smells on the energy consumption of mobile applications. In *Information and Software Technology* 105: 43–55.

Pauwels, Koen et al. 2009. Dashboards as a service: Why, what, how, and what research is needed? *Journal of Service Research* 12(2): 175–189.

Pazzani, Michael J. et al. 2007. Content-based recommendation systems. In *The Adaptive Web: Methods and Strategies of Web Personalization*, 325–341. Berlin, Heidelberg: Springer Berlin Heidelberg.

Phillips, Dewanne M. et al. 2018. An architecture, system engineering, and acquisition approach for space system software resiliency. *Information and Software Technology* 94: 150–164.

PowerTop (n.d.). https://01.org/powertop/. Accessed 07 October 2021.

Rahman, Azizah Abdul et al. 2017. Review on dashboard application from managerial perspective. In *2017 International Conference on Research and Innovation in Information Systems (ICRIIS)*. Piscataway: IEEE.

Rogers, Robert D. et al. 1995. Costs of a predictible switch between simple cognitive tasks. *Journal of Experimental Psychology: General* 124(2): 207–231.

Ruparelia, Nayan B. 2010. Software development lifecycle models. *ACM SIGSOFT Software Engineering Notes* 35(3): 8–13.

Sarwar, Badrul et al. 2001. Item-based collaborative filtering recommendation algorithms. In *Proceedings of ACM World Wide Web Conference* 1.

Savoie, Michael. 2012. *Building successful information systems: Five best practices to ensure organizational effectiveness and profitability*. Business Expert Press.

Schafer J. Ben et al. 2007. Collaborative filtering recommender systems. In *The adaptive web: Methods and strategies of web personalization*, 291–324. Berlin, Heidelberg: Springer Berlin Heidelberg.

Sidhu, Brahmaleen Kaur et al. 2022. A machine learning approach to software model refactoring. *International Journal of Computers and Applications* 44(2): 166–177.

Silva, Dennis et al. 2016. A hybrid approach for test case prioritization and selection. In *2016 IEEE Congress on Evolutionary Computation (CEC)*. Piscataway: IEEE.

Solingen, Rini van et al. 1999. The goal/question/metric method: A practical guide for quality improvement of software development.

Sultan, Khalid et al. 2008. Catalog of metrics for assessing security risks of software throughout the software development life cycle. In *2008 International Conference on Information Security and Assurance (ISA 2008)*, 461–465. Piscataway: IEEE.

Thierauf, Robert J. 1991. *Executive information systems: a guide for senior management and MIS professionals*. Quorum Books.

Thung, Ferdian et al. 2013. Automatic recommendation of API methods from feature requests. In *Proceedings of the 28th IEEE/ACM International Conference on Automated Software Engineering*. ASE'13, 290–300. Silicon Valley: IEEE Press.

Tiwari, Vivek et al. 1994. Power analysis of embedded software: A first step towards software power minimization. *IEEE Transactions on Very Large Scale Integration (VLSI) Systems* 2(4): 437–445.

Tiwari, Vivek et al. 1996. Instruction level power analysis and optimization of software. In *Technologies for wireless computing*, 139–154. Boston: Springer.

Tsoumakas, Grigorios et al. 2009. Multi-label classification: An overview. *International Journal of Data Warehousing and Mining* 3: 1–13.

Wang, Hulong et al. 2021. User-based collaborative filtering algorithm design and implementation. *Journal of Physics: Conference Series* 1757(1): 012168.

Wang, Junjie et al. 2020. Context-aware in-process crowdworker recommendation. In *Proceedings of the ACM/IEEE 42nd International Conference on Software Engineering*. ICSE '20, 1535–1546. Seoul: Association for Computing Machinery.

Wieruch, Robin. 2022. *Mediator component in react*. https://www.robinwieruch.de/react-mediator-component/. Accessed 25 February 2022.

Xie, Wenkai et al. 2020. API method recommendation via explicit matching of functionality verb phrases. In *Proceedings of the 28th ACM Joint Meeting on European Software Engineering Conference and Symposium on the Foundations of Software Engineering*. ESEC/FSE 2020, 1015–1026. Virtual Event, USA: Association for Computing Machinery.

Yadav, Harikesh Bahadur et al. 2013. Defects prediction of early phases of software development life cycle using fuzzy logic. In *Confluence 2013: The Next Generation Information Technology Summit (4th International Conference)*, 2–6. IET.

Yigitbasioglu, Ogan M. et al. 2012. A review of dashboards in performance management: Implications for design and research. *International Journal of Accounting Information Systems* 13(1): 41–59.

Zhang, Huazhe et al. 2016. Maximizing performance under a power cap: A comparison of hardware, software, and hybrid techniques. *ACM SIGPLAN Notices* 51(4): 545–559.

Zhang, Jian et al. 2018a. Semantically enhanced tag recommendation for software CQAs via deep learning. In *Proceedings of the 40th International Conference on Software Engineering: Companion Proceeedings*. ICSE '18, 294–295. Gothenburg: Association for Computing Machinery.

Zhang, Min-Ling et al. 2014. A review on multi-label learning algorithms. *IEEE Transactions on Knowledge and Data Engineering* 26: 1819–1837.

Zhang, Youjun et al. 2018b. A novel method of processing class imbalance and its application in transaction fraud detection. In *2018 IEEE/ACM 5th International Conference on Big Data Computing Applications and Technologies (BDCAT)*, 152–159. Piscataway: IEEE.

Printed in the United States
by Baker & Taylor Publisher Services